HBR Guide to
Unlocking
Creativity

Harvard Business Review Guides

Arm yourself with the advice you need to succeed on the job, from the most trusted brand in business. Packed with how-to essentials from leading experts, the HBR Guides provide smart answers to your most pressing work challenges.

The titles include:

HBR Guide for Women at Work

HBR Guide to AI Basics for Managers

HBR Guide to Beating Burnout

HBR Guide to Being a Great Boss

HBR Guide to Being More Productive

HBR Guide to Better Business Writing

HBR Guide to Better Mental Health at Work

HBR Guide to Building Your Business Case

HBR Guide to Buying a Small Business

HBR Guide to Changing Your Career

HBR Guide to Coaching Employees

HBR Guide to Collaborative Teams

HBR Guide to Critical Thinking

HBR Guide to Data Analytics Basics for Managers

HBR Guide to Dealing with Conflict

HBR Guide to Delivering Effective Feedback

HBR Guide to Designing Your Retirement

HBR Guide to Emotional Intelligence

HBR Guide to Finance Basics for Managers

HBR Guide to Getting the Mentoring You Need

HBR Guide to Getting the Right Job

HBR Guide to Getting the Right Work Done

HBR Guide to Leading Teams

HBR Guide to Making Better Decisions

HBR Guide to Making Every Meeting Matter

HBR Guide to Managing Flexible Work

HBR Guide to Managing Strategic Initiatives

HBR Guide to Managing Stress at Work

HBR Guide to Managing Up and Across

HBR Guide to Motivating People

HBR Guide to Negotiating

HBR Guide to Networking

HBR Guide to Office Politics

HBR Guide to Performance Management

HBR Guide to Persuasive Presentations

HBR Guide to Project Management

HBR Guide to Remote Work

HBR Guide to Setting Your Strategy

HBR Guide to Smarter Networking

HBR Guide to Thinking Strategically

HBR Guide to Unlocking Creativity

HBR Guide to Work-Life Balance

HBR Guide to Your Professional Growth

HBR Guide to **Unlocking Creativity**

HARVARD BUSINESS REVIEW PRESS

Boston, Massachusetts

The web addresses referenced in this book were live and correct at the time of the book's publication but may be subject to change.

Library of Congress Cataloging-in-Publication Data

Names: Harvard Business Review Press, issuing body.
Title: HBR guide to unlocking creativity / Harvard Business Review.
Other titles: Harvard business review guide to unlocking creativity | Harvard business review guides.
Description: Boston, Massachusetts : Harvard Business Review Press, [2023] | Series: HBR guides | Includes index. |
Identifiers: LCCN 2022057871 (print) | LCCN 2022057872 (ebook) | ISBN 9781647825065 (paperback) | ISBN 9781647825072 (epub)
Subjects: LCSH: Creative ability in business. | Success in business.
Classification: LCC HD53 .H384 2023 (print) | LCC HD53 (ebook) | DDC 650.1—dc23/eng/20230224
LC record available at https://lccn.loc.gov/2022057871
LC ebook record available at https://lccn.loc.gov/2022057872

ISBN: 978-1-64782-506-5

eISBN: 978-1-64782-507-2

The paper used in this publication meets the requirements of the American National Standard for Permanence of Paper for Publications and Documents in Libraries and Archives Z39.48-1992.

What You'll Learn

When you picture a creative person, who pops into your head? Is it a well-known CEO? A famous performer, artist, scientist, or architect? Or maybe someone you know comes to mind—a coworker on the design team, an old classmate who was always effortlessly fashionable, or your friend whose social posts get the most likes?

Here's the thing: These individuals are impressive and inspiring, but they don't own a monopoly on creativity. You don't need to be the next Steve Jobs, Beyoncé, Jack Ma, or Zaha Hadid to be an innovator, nor do you need to work in a certain department or industry. There's less that separates you from "creatives" than you might think, and no matter who you are or what you do in your job, you can learn to unlock your own inherent creative capacity and bring it to your work.

No matter what business you're in, you need new perspectives and novel ways of doing things to keep pace with your competitors and set yourself apart. That's why a creative mindset is now one of the most sought-after traits for leaders—without it, your organization will be stuck in neutral. Creativity makes innovation possible.

You're not alone if you feel some hesitancy around proposing something different or encouraging others to be creative. Many of us—because of our culture, education, or work experience—have been taught that logical and practical thinking are the keys to success. Too often, we may feel that managers and organizational culture can stifle our best new ideas. Many creative approaches never see the light of day, because they don't fit easily into a P&L. But the level of complexity and the speed of change in business today are too high; you cannot simply recycle the old ways of doing things. You can—and must!—set the right conditions for creativity to thrive around you. And you need to be part of the process yourself.

The *HBR Guide to Unlocking Creativity* will help you and your team change how you think, innovate together, and achieve original results that will make *you* an inspiration to others.

You will learn to:

- Overcome the fears that block your best ideas

- Understand when to take a break and when to push through

- Balance creativity with productivity

- Brainstorm for better questions—not just solutions

- Revive your imagination when you're stressed or just in a rut

- Model curiosity for your team

- Understand when to switch from divergent thinking to convergent thinking

- Give and receive feedback about creative work

- Collaborate for creativity in remote and hybrid workplaces

- Cultivate the psychological safety needed for unguarded expression

- Use design thinking to generate new solutions

- Build a culture of originality

- Bring breakthrough ideas to life

Contents

Contents

SECTION TWO

Brainstorming and Beyond

SECTION THREE

Creative Collaboration

Contents

SECTION FOUR

Make Your Organization More Creative

Contents

Creativity: Not Just for Creatives

We all know the feeling of entering a room where all the joy and exuberance of creativity and open-minded thinking dried up years ago. We feel it the most when we're dealing with old systems and giant bureaucracies— things like filing an insurance claim or applying for an extended travel visa. The experience is withering and exhausting, and we feel a mix of sympathy and derision for its enforcers: those robotic paper-pushers who never seem to stray from their scripts or fail to apply outdated rules.

Most of us today, luckily, work in organizations where innovation is encouraged and celebrated. Even so, that creativity-crushing feeling creeps into our jobs all too often. The forces that smother creativity and lead to rigid, defensive feelings are quiet and sly. They might show up as a manager who steals your good ideas, as strategy sessions that are exercises in groupthink, or as a culture of busyness that leaves no time for deep thinking. Everyday problems such as these are likely making it harder for your team to generate original ideas and new solutions. And the longer you spend in this kind of culture, the more your own creative juices are going to dry up too.

The good news is that there are steps you can take, today, to rekindle your creativity. What's more, any team or organization can do the same. The chapters in this guide bring together some of HBR's most practical, actionable, and thought-provoking articles on these topics. They provide a variety of approaches to unlocking creativity in yourself and your team so that you can see things differently, spark innovation, and solve tough problems. Throughout the book, you'll see that creativity experts and researchers agree on several observations:

1. There aren't "creative people" and "uncreative people." Everyone is born creative and can be creative given the right opportunities.

2. Creativity seldom springs forth from solitary light-bulb moments. It's more likely to come from creative collaboration that combines ideas and insights in unexpected ways.

3. Creativity fuels innovation. It allows you and your team to see beyond what exists now to

what might be, helping your organization evolve and grow.

Beyond this starting point, though, you'll see that there is no single, foolproof playbook for creativity. Some of the authors in this guide will encourage you to reflect. They'll ask you to examine yourself and the mindsets that might be holding you back in your efforts to be creative—whether that's a fear of failure, being in a rut, or just working under constant stress. Others will urge you to look at what's impeding creative collaboration on your team. You might, for example, be running the wrong kind of brainstorm, struggle to ensure psychological safety on your team, or simply have too many similar people in your meetings.

Start thinking differently by letting yourself read this guide in any order—don't just start at page 1 and read it front to back. Take a look at the table of contents, and read the chapter titles. If you see a title that catches your eye, skip ahead and then jump back. Underline what is important to you, take notes, and mark up the pages. If the book helps you come up with a single breakthrough—or if it helps your team get unstuck or reach a better outcome—then your time reading this guide is well spent.

The articles in section 1, "Unleash Your Creativity," will help you assess yourself and understand where you are on your journey of creative growth. It begins with "Reclaim Your Creative Confidence," a chapter by two d.school professors who show you how to examine and get over the fears that are blocking your best ideas.

Throughout the section, you'll learn to give your brain the exercise it needs, how to spark creativity when you're stressed or in a rut, and why you need to look outside your industry for fresh solutions.

The right kind of brainstorming can generate incredible new ideas—but the wrong kind can actually produce fewer good ideas than people working by themselves. Section 2, "Brainstorming and Beyond," encourages you to move past the old standard tactics and learn about brainstorming for questions, storythinking, brainswarming, and ways to make virtual brainstorming even more effective than in-person techniques. Spend extra time in this section if you want to add a few more idea-generation skills to your repertoire.

Ultimately, getting good ideas onto the whiteboard is only a start. To put creative solutions into action, your team needs to learn to innovate together. Section 3, "Creative Collaboration," shows you how to set the conditions for team creativity, how to balance psychological safety with diverse viewpoints, and how to give feedback to others about their creative work. Read all the chapters in this section if you already have plenty of ideas but want to combine, refine, and hone them.

The final section, "Make Your Organization More Creative," zooms out to look at how small changes in culture can have a huge impact on problem-solving. These chapters explore how everyone in a company—from individual contributors to managers to leaders—can adjust their approach to celebrate curiosity, adopt a growth mindset around innovation, and build a culture of originality.

Late in this guide, organizational psychologist and creativity guru Adam Grant describes his mission to find innovators in what he thought was the least likely organization. "If there's one place on earth where originality goes to die, I'd managed to find it. I was charged with unleashing innovation and change in the ultimate bastion of bureaucracy. It was a place where people accepted defaults without question, followed rules without explanation, and clung to traditions and technologies long after they'd become obsolete: the U.S. Navy." Amazingly, though, when Grant continued to explore there, he found much more creativity than he had expected. These creative solutions weren't coming from the top down—they were bubbling up from a network of original thinkers throughout the organization, and leadership was encouraging these thinkers to question long-held assumptions.

Even in the biggest, most complex companies, creativity can start with you. And the higher you are on the org chart, the more you can enable others to reach their own creative potential. If your organization—or even just a dull standing meeting—feels like a creative wasteland today, don't assume that it can't become a grove of innovative ideas tomorrow. Read on, and start watering the soil now.

SECTION ONE

Unleash Your Creativity

CHAPTER 1

Reclaim Your Creative Confidence

by Tom Kelley and David Kelley

Most people are born creative. As children, we revel in imaginary play, ask outlandish questions, draw blobs and call them dinosaurs. But over time, because of socialization and formal education, a lot of us start to stifle those impulses. We learn to be warier of judgment, more cautious, more analytical. The world seems to be divided into *creatives* and *noncreatives*, and too many people consciously or unconsciously resign themselves to the latter category.

Adapted from an article in *Harvard Business Review*, December 2012 (product #R1212K).

And yet we know that creativity is essential to success in any discipline or industry. According to an IBM survey of chief executives around the world, it's the most sought-after trait in leaders. No one can deny that creative thinking has enabled the rise and continued success of countless companies, from startups to stalwarts.

Students often come to Stanford University's "d.school" (which was founded by one of us—David—and is formally known as the Hasso Plattner Institute of Design) to develop their creativity. Clients work with IDEO, our design and innovation consultancy, for the same reason. But along the way, we've learned that our job isn't to *teach* them creativity. It's to help them *rediscover* their creative confidence—the natural ability to come up with new ideas and the courage to try them out. We do this by giving them strategies to get past four fears that hold most of us back:

- Fear of the messy unknown

- Fear of being judged

- Fear of the first step

- Fear of losing control

Easier said than done, you might argue. But we know it's possible for people to overcome even their most deep-seated fears. Consider the work of Albert Bandura, a world-renowned psychologist and Stanford professor. In one series of early experiments, he helped people conquer lifelong snake phobias by guiding them through a series of increasingly demanding interactions.

They would start by watching a snake through a two-way mirror. Once comfortable with that, they'd progress to observing it through an open door, then to watching someone else touch the snake, then to touching it themselves through a heavy leather glove, and, finally, in a few hours, to touching it with their own bare hands. Bandura calls this process of experiencing one small success after another "guided mastery." The people who went through it weren't just cured of a debilitating fear they had assumed was untreatable. They also had less anxiety and more success in other parts of their lives, taking up new and potentially frightening activities like horseback riding and public speaking. They tried harder, persevered longer, and had more resilience in the face of failure. They had gained a new confidence in their ability to attain what they set out to do.

We've used much the same approach over the past 30 years to help people transcend the fears that block their creativity. You break challenges down into small steps and then build confidence by succeeding on one step after another. Creativity is something you practice, not just a talent you're born with. The process may feel a little uncomfortable at first, but—as the snake phobics learned—the discomfort quickly fades away and is replaced with new confidence and capabilities.

Fear of the Messy Unknown

Creative thinking in business begins with having empathy for your customers (whether they're internal or external), and you can't get that sitting behind a desk. Yes, we know it's cozy in your office. Everything is reassuringly familiar, information comes from predictable sources, contradictory data is weeded out and ignored. But out in the world, it's more chaotic. You have to deal with unexpected findings, with uncertainty, and with irrational people who say things you don't want to hear. But that is where you find insights—and creative breakthroughs. Venturing forth in pursuit of learning, even without a hypothesis, can open you up to new information and help you discover nonobvious needs. Otherwise, you risk simply reconfirming ideas you've already had or waiting for others—your customers, your boss, or even your competitors—to tell you what to do.

At the d.school, we routinely assign students to do this sort of anthropological fieldwork—to get out of their comfort zones and into the world—until, suddenly, they start doing it on their own. Consider a computer scientist, two engineers, and an MBA student, all of whom took the Design for Extreme Affordability class taught by Stanford business school professor Jim Patell. The students eventually realized that they couldn't complete their group project—to research and design a low-cost incubator for newborn babies in the developing world—while living in safe suburban California. So they gathered their courage and visited rural Nepal. Talking with families and doctors firsthand, they learned that the babies in gravest danger were those born prematurely in areas far from hospitals. Nepalese villagers didn't need a cheaper incubator at the hospital—they needed a fail-safe way to keep babies warm when they lived far from doctors who could do so effectively. Those insights led the team to design a miniature "sleeping bag" with a pouch containing a special heat-storing wax. The Embrace Infant Warmer costs 99% less than a traditional incubator and can maintain the right temperature for up to six hours with no external power source. The innovation has the potential to save millions of low-birth-weight and premature babies every year, and it came about only because the team members were willing to throw themselves into unfamiliar territory.

Another example comes from Akshay Kothari and Ankit Gupta, two students who took the d.school's Launchpad course. The class required them to start a company from scratch by the end of the 10-week academic quarter. Both were self-described "geeks"—technically brilliant, deeply analytical, and definitely shy. But they opted to work on their project—an elegant news reader for the then newly released iPad—off campus in a Palo Alto café where they'd be surrounded by potential users. Getting over the awkwardness of approaching strangers, Kothari gathered feedback by asking café patrons to experiment with his prototypes. Gupta coded hundreds of small variations to be tested each day—changing everything from interaction patterns to the size of a button. In a matter of weeks, he and Kothari rapidly iterated their way to a successful product. "We went from people saying, 'This is crap,'" says Kothari, "to 'Is this app preloaded on every iPad?'" The result—Pulse News—received public praise from Steve Jobs at a worldwide developer's conference only a few months later and is one of the original 50 apps in Apple's App Store Hall of Fame.

It's not just entrepreneurs and product developers who should get into the mess. Senior managers must

TACKLING THE MESS, RIGHT NOW

by Caroline O'Connor and Sarah Stein Greenberg

You can work up the confidence to tackle the big fears that hold most of us back by starting small. Here are a few ways to get comfortable with venturing into the messy unknown. The list gets increasingly challenging, but you can follow the first two suggestions without even leaving your desk.

- *Lurk in online forums.* Listen in as potential customers share information, air grievances, and ask questions—it's the virtual equivalent of hanging around a popular café. You're not looking for evaluations of features or cost; you're searching for clues about people's concerns and desires.

- *Pick up the phone and call your own company's customer service line.* Walk through the experience as if you were a customer, noting how your problem is handled and how you're feeling along the way.

- *Seek out an unexpected expert.* What does the receptionist in your building know about your firm's customer experience? If you use a car service for work travel, what insights do the drivers have about your firm? If you're in health care, talk to a medical assistant, not a doctor. If you make a physical product, ask a repair person to tell you about common failure areas.

- *Act like a spy.* Take a magazine and a pair of headphones to a store or an industry conference (or, if your customers are internal, a break room or lunch area). Pretend to read while you observe. Watch as if you were a kid trying to understand what is going on. How are people interacting with your offering? What can you glean from their body language?

- *Casually interview a customer or potential customer.* After you've gotten more comfortable venturing out, try this: Write down a few open-ended questions about your product or service. Go to a place where your customers tend to gather, find someone you'd be comfortable approaching, and say you'd like to ask a few questions. If the person refuses? No problem, just try someone else. Eventually you'll find someone who's dying to talk to you. Press for more detail with every question. Even if you think you understand, ask, "Why is that?" or "Can you tell me more about that?" Get people to dig into their own underlying assumptions.

Caroline O'Connor is a lecturer at the Hasso Plattner Institute of Design. **Sarah Stein Greenberg** is its managing director.

also hear directly from anyone affected by their decisions. For instance, midway through a management off-site that IDEO held for ConAgra Foods, the executives broke away from their upscale conference rooms to explore gritty Detroit neighborhoods, where you can go miles without seeing a grocery store. They personally observed how the residents of these neighborhoods reacted to food products, and the executives spoke with an urban farmer who hopes to turn abandoned lots into community gardens. Now, according to Al Bolles, ConAgra's executive vice president of research, quality, and innovation, such behavior is common at the company. "A few years ago," he says, "it was hard to pry my executive team away from the office. But now we venture out and get onto our customers' home turf to get insights about what they really need."

Fear of Being Judged

If the scribbling, singing, dancing kindergartner symbolizes unfettered creative expression, then the awkward teenager represents the opposite: someone who cares—*deeply*—about what other people think. It takes only a few years to develop that fear of judgment, but it stays with us throughout our adult lives, often constraining our careers. Most of us accept that when we are learning, say, to ski, others will see us fall down until practice pays off. But we can't risk our business-world ego in the same way. As a result, we self-edit, killing potentially creative ideas because we're afraid our bosses or peers will see us fail. We stick to safe solutions or suggestions. We hang back, allowing others to take risks. But we can't be creative if we are constantly censoring ourselves.

Half the battle is to resist judging *yourself*. If you can listen to your own intuition and embrace more of your own ideas (good and bad), you're already partway to overcoming this fear. So take baby steps, as Bandura's clients did. Instead of letting thoughts run through your head and down the drain, capture them systematically in some form of idea notebook. Keep a whiteboard and marker in the shower. Schedule daily "white space" in your calendar, where your only task is to think or take a walk and daydream. When you try to generate ideas, shoot for 100 instead of 10. Defer your own judgment, and you'll be surprised at how many ideas you have—and like—by the end of the week.

Also, try using new language when you give feedback, and encourage your collaborators to do the same. At the d.school, our feedback typically starts with "I like . . ." and moves on to "I wish . . ." instead of just passing judgment with putdowns like "That will never work." (See chapter 18 of this book for more on how to give and receive feedback about creative work.) Opening with the positives and then using the first person for suggestions signals that "this is just my opinion, and I want to help"—a message that makes listeners more receptive to your ideas.

We recently worked with Air New Zealand to reinvent the customer experience for its long-distance flights. As a highly regulated industry, airlines tend toward conservatism. To overcome the cultural norm of skepticism and caution, we started with a workshop aimed at generating wild ideas. Executives brainstormed and prototyped a dozen unconventional (and some seemingly impractical) concepts, including harnesses that hold people standing up, groups of seats facing one another around a table, and even hammocks and bunk beds. With everyone coming up with these ideas, no one was scared of being judged. This willingness to consider wild notions and defer judgment eventually led the Air New Zealand team to a creative breakthrough: the Skycouch, a lie-flat seat for economy class. At first, it seemed impossible that such a seat could be made without enlarging its footprint (seats in business and first-class cabins take up much more space), but the new design does just that: A heavily padded section swings up like a footrest to transform an airline row into a futonlike platform that a couple can lie down on together. The Skycouch is now featured on a number of Air New Zealand's international flights, and the company has won several industry awards as a result.

Fear of the First Step

Even when we want to embrace our creative ideas, acting on them presents its own challenges. Creative efforts are hardest at the beginning. The writer faces the blank page; the teacher, the start of school; businesspeople, the first day of a new project. In a broader sense, we're also talking about fear of charting a new path or breaking out of your predictable workflow. To overcome this inertia, you need more than good ideas. You need to stop planning and just get started—and the best way to do that is to stop focusing on the huge overall task and find a small piece you can tackle right away.

Bestselling writer Anne Lamott expertly captures this idea in a story from her childhood. Her brother had been assigned a school report about birds, but he waited to start on it until the night before it was due. He was near tears, overwhelmed by the task ahead, until his father gave him some wise advice: "Bird by bird, buddy. Just take it bird by bird." In a business context, you can push yourself to take the first step by asking, What is the low-cost experiment? What's the quickest, cheapest way to make progress toward the larger goal?

Or give yourself a ridiculous deadline, as John Keefe, a d.school alum and a senior editor at radio station WNYC, did after a colleague complained that her mom had to wait at city bus stops never knowing when the next bus would come. If you worked for New York City Transit Authority and your boss asked you to solve that problem, how soon would you promise to get a system up and running? Six weeks? Ten? Keefe, who *doesn't* work for the transit authority, said, "Give me till the end of the day." He bought an 800 number, figured out how to access real-time bus data, and linked it to text-to-speech technology. Within 24 hours, he had set up a service that allowed bus riders to call in, input their bus stop number, and hear the location of the approaching bus. Keefe applies the same fearless attitude to his work at WNYC. "The most effective way I've found to practice design thinking is by showing, not telling," he explains.

Another example of the start-simple strategy comes from an IDEO project to develop a new dashboard feature for a European luxury car. To test their ideas, designers videotaped an existing car and then used digital

effects to layer on proposed features. The rapid prototyping process took less than a week. When the team
showed the video to our client, he laughed. "Last time we
did something like this," he said, "we built a prototype
car, which took almost a year and cost over a million dol-
lars. Then we took a video of it. You skipped the car and
went straight to the video."

Our mantra is "Don't get ready, get started!" The first
step will seem much less daunting if you make it a tiny
one and force yourself to do it *right now*. Rather than
stalling and allowing your anxiety to build, just start
inching toward the snake.

Fear of Losing Control

Confidence doesn't simply mean believing that your ideas
are good. It means having the humility to let go of ideas
that aren't working and to accept good ideas from other
people. When you abandon the status quo and work collaboratively, you sacrifice control over your product, your
team, and your business. But the creative gains can more
than compensate. Again, you can start small. If you're
facing a tough challenge, try calling a meeting with people fresh to the topic. Or break the routine of a weekly
meeting by letting the most junior person in the room
set the agenda and lead it. Look for opportunities to cede
control and to leverage different perspectives.

That's exactly what Bonny Simi, director of airport
planning at JetBlue Airways, did after an ice storm
closed John F. Kennedy International Airport for a six-
hour stretch—and disrupted the airline's flight service
for the next six days. Everyone knew there were op-

erational problems to be fixed, but no one knew exactly what to do. Fresh from a d.school course, Simi suggested that JetBlue brainstorm solutions from the bottom up rather than the top down. First, she gathered a team of 120 frontline employees—pilots, flight attendants, dispatchers, ramp workers, crew schedulers, and other staff members—for just one day. Then she mapped out their disruption recovery actions (using yellow Post-it notes) and the challenges they faced (using pink ones). By the end of the day, Bonny's grassroots task force had reached new insights—and resolve. The distributed team then spent the next few months working through more than a thousand pink Post-it notes to creatively solve each problem. By admitting that the answers lay in the collective, Simi did more than she could ever have done alone. And JetBlue now recovers from major disruptions significantly faster than it did before.

Our own experience with the open innovation platform OpenIDEO is another case in point. Its launch was scary in two ways: First, we were starting a public conversation that could quickly get out of hand; second, we were admitting that we don't have all the answers. But we were ready, like Bandura's folks with snake phobias, to take a bigger leap—to touch the snake. And we soon discovered the benefits. As of this writing, the OpenIDEO community includes about 30,000 people from 170 countries. The people involved may never meet in person, but together they've already made a difference on dozens of initiatives—from helping revitalize cities in economic decline to prototyping ultrasound services for expectant mothers in Colombia. We've learned that no matter what group you're in or where you work, there are always more ideas outside than inside. For people with backgrounds as diverse as those of Kothari, Gupta, Keefe, and Simi, fear—of the messy unknown, of judgment, of taking the first step, or of letting go—could have blocked the path to innovation. But instead, they worked to overcome their fears, rediscovered their creative confidence, and made a difference. As Hungarian essayist György Konrád once said, "Courage is only the accumulation of small steps." So don't wait at the starting line. Let go of your fears, and begin practicing creative confidence today.

———————

Tom Kelley is the coauthor of *Creative Confidence* and a partner at IDEO, a global design and innovation firm. **David Kelley** is the founder and chairman of IDEO and the founder of the Hasso Plattner Institute of Design at Stanford.

CHAPTER 2

Train Your Brain to Be More Creative

by Bas Korsten

Great athletes train their bodies for days, weeks, and years to whip them into peak performance. Why, then, wouldn't a creator do the same with their brain? Think about it. Your brain needs fuel, and it needs to be stretched to create those "OMG!" moments on demand.

I've spent more than two decades (and counting) in the advertising industry, and contrary to popular belief, creativity isn't inherent. You have to hone it. Over time, I've figured out what I need to do to get ideas flowing freely, and much of that insight comes from my interest in neuroscience. The more we learn about the workings

Adapted from content posted on Ascend, hbr.org, June 17, 2021.

of our gray matter, the better we can train it, control it, and make it do what we want.

Here a few things that have worked for me over the years.

Engaging with Nature

Many studies have shown that spending time in nature makes us more creative. Looking at trees and leaves—instead of our electronic devices—reduces our anxiety, lowers our heart rates, soothes us, and allows our brains to make connections more easily.

By spending time in nature, I'm not referring to a trek in the wilderness. Walking in an urban green space for just 25 minutes can quiet our brains and help us switch into autopilot mode. According to the *British Journal of Sports Medicine*, this state sparks our awareness of the present and fuels imagination. We are better able to connect existing notions, thoughts, and images to form a new, relevant, and usable concept.

Make disconnecting a priority. Take a walk in your neighborhood park, stroll along the beach, or just add plants to your balcony and spend some time out there. For me, walking my dog works. You'll feel the benefits of moving away from screens almost immediately.

Meditation

I know you've heard this a million times: Meditation clears our minds of jumbled thoughts, and it gives our brains the space to observe and reflect, improving task concentration and enhancing our ability to make smart decisions.

But did you know that meditation also puts the entire brain to work?

Many believe that creativity uses your right brain, and that more analytical tasks trigger the left. But in fact, neuroscientists have found that creativity draws on your *entire* brain—and meditation can you give you access to it.

This intentional practice can be as simple as closing your eyes and focusing on your breath. Headspace, the popular meditation app, even has guided meditations specifically meant to inspire creativity. When we intentionally pause in awareness, we allow our minds the freedom and space to be still and creative. I practice meditation between meetings. I find a quiet space, focus on my breathing, and get my brain into an alpha state—the wakeful state of relaxation. This allows me to disconnect from my initial ideas (after all, the human brain is hardwired to take the path of least resistance) and create new pathways in my mind.

Physical Movement

Steve Jobs was a big advocate for walking meetings for a reason. Moving around has been linked to increased performance on creative tests. Exercising releases endorphins—chemicals our bodies produce to relieve stress and pain. When we are less stressed, our brains venture into more fruitful territory.

In fact, one article compared the chemical that our brain releases during physical activity to Miracle-Gro, the water-soluble plant food that helps grow bigger, healthier plants.[1] Moving around is super simple to do, especially when you're working at home. I often attend meetings while cycling on a stationary bike or plan short walks in between meetings. (You can do these in an office too.)

Try to add workout time on your calendar, and make sure not to skip it. If you feel you don't have time for a dedicated workout, block 20 minutes on your calendar and spend that time doing stretches at your desk. Find a routine that works for you.

Connections with Different Kinds of People

For deliberate sources of inspiration, not enough can be said about diversity. Remember the brain and its predisposition to take the lazy way out? Diversity makes the brain work harder by challenging stereotypes. In addition, Ernest T. Pascarella and his coauthors published an article in the *Journal of College Student Development* that showed that "exposure to diversity experiences might foster the development of more complex forms of thought, including the ability to think critically."

I make it a point to surround myself with people who come from backgrounds different from mine, because their perspectives are a catalyst for creative thinking. Contrasting opinions spark new possibilities and allow us to make connections we hadn't seen before, leading to better decisions. There was something to be said about Abraham Lincoln's filling his cabinet with a "team of rivals." At my agency, we've set up an "inspiration council," which brings together our people from various regions, cultures, genders, and more, to initiate these kind of discussions.

The distributed working model has made it even easier to bring people together. I recommend using social media channels like LinkedIn and Instagram to follow and connect with people who have backgrounds and experiences that diverge from your own. Don't limit yourself by geography when you're reaching out to someone or expanding your network. We are much better at creative problem-solving when we don't have the comfort of knowing what to expect. We can become too comfortable if we only surround ourselves with people just like us. (See more about how diversity on teams improves creative performance in chapter 15 of this guide.)

Use these four principles from neuroscience to give your brain the exercise that it needs. These practices will get you out of any rut. Or prevent you from getting into one in the first place.

———

Bas Korsten is the Global Chief Creative Officer at Wunderman Thompson.

NOTE

1. Helen O'Callaghan, "'Physical Activity Is Like Miracle-Gro': Simple Steps to Boost Your Brain as You Age," *Irish Examiner*, March 26, 2011, www.irishexaminer.com/lifestyle/healthandwellbeing/arid-40251431.html.

CHAPTER 3

How to Spark Creativity When You're in a Rut

by Priscilla Claman

Remember your first day at work? You were excited. There were new people to meet, new skills to be learned, new processes or products to understand.

If you are like most people, something else was different then—you. When you weren't sure or didn't understand, you asked questions, persistently. You compared what you were supposed to do on this job with what you had done in the past, and you made suggestions. You observed what your new colleagues were doing and

---

Adapted from content posted on hbr.org, April 19, 2017 (product #H03M4Y).

evaluated what you saw. As a new person, you felt entitled to look at things differently and ask questions—that was a sign of your creativity.

Hiring managers look for people who can come in, assess a function, and recommend changes. They know that new people with new ideas can bring energy and creativity to a workplace, no matter what the level of their job is.

Everyone has creativity when confronted with new problems to solve or new ideas to think about. The first few months on any job can be exhausting as well as exciting, so people naturally set their work lives into a groove after a while. In time, that groove can turn into a rut. And people in a rut can develop habits that kill off their own creativity.

Are you in a creativity-destroying rut? Ask yourself these five questions:

- Is there a recurring pattern to your workdays— what you do, whom you meet with?

- Do you feel you have to agree with your colleagues and bosses to get along?

- Do you see obstacles everywhere to new ideas and new ways of doing things?

- Do you find yourself saying, "That won't work. It's been tried too many times before."

- Do you think, "It doesn't matter what I do, really. They don't care." Even when you're not sure who "they" are?

If you answered yes to these, you may have allowed yourself to accept thought and behavior patterns that are undermining your creativity. Of course, there may indeed be obstacles everywhere, and maybe "they" don't care, but that's not what is important. What's important is that you get those creative juices flowing again. Here are some suggestions to rekindle your creativity:

- **Think new.** Meet new people at work. Talk to new clients. Ask for new assignments. Learn something new—a new program, a new product, a new process. If you do something new every month, you won't just add to your résumé; you'll reinvigorate yourself.

- **Look for intersections.** A lot of creativity occurs at the crossroads of different people and different ideas. Look for places where your department intersects with other departments. What do they do that helps your department? What gets in the way? Volunteer for any cross-functional activity you can, whether it's a day of service or a new product team.

- **Capitalize on obstacles.** Remember that phrase "Necessity is the mother of invention"? Well, it's true. Every obstacle is an opportunity for research and analysis. Why is it there? Whom does it serve? What are its effects? What are other ways of getting the results you're looking for? Start by selecting obstacles you can change, and move on from there. You'll build a reputation as a problem solver.

31

- **Share what you know.** Nothing makes you clarify your thoughts like sharing what you know, whether it's in a blog post or at a training session or as a mentor. Look for those opportunities. Volunteer. You'll be surprised at how engaged and happy these efforts make you feel.

There is an overall way of thinking about the difference between habits that sap your creativity and those that make your creativity shine. Habits that sap your creativity leave you just "doing stuff." There's no *you* in the job, only transactions. When you develop habits that enhance your on-the-job creativity, you make the job your own. In a way, you are *above* the job, making it better, more interesting, and more effective and contributing your best self. That's the difference between someone who is just an employee and someone who is a real professional.

Priscilla Claman is president of Career Strategies, Inc., a Boston-area firm offering career coaching to individuals and career management services to organizations.

CHAPTER 4

Schedule Your Breaks to Keep Creativity Flowing

by Jackson G. Lu, Modupe Akinola, and Malia Mason

Imagine that on a Friday afternoon, before finishing up work to start your weekend, you are asked to solve two problems that require creative thinking. Which of the following approaches do you take?

- Spend the first half of your time attempting the first problem and the second half of your time attempting the second.

Adapted from "To Be More Creative, Schedule Your Breaks" on hbr.org, May 10, 2017 (product #H03MY1).

- Alternate between the two problems at a regular, predetermined interval (perhaps switching every five minutes).

- Switch between the problems at your own discretion.

If you are like the hundreds of people to whom we posed this question, you would choose to switch between the two problems at your own discretion. After all, this approach offers maximum autonomy and flexibility, enabling you to change tracks from one problem to the other when you feel stuck.

But if coming up with creative answers is your goal, this approach may not be optimal. Instead, switching between the problems at a regular, predetermined interval is likely to yield the best results, according to research we published in *Organizational Behavior and Human Decision Processes*.

Why might switching at your own volition, the approach most participants in our study took, not generate the most creative outcomes? Because when attempting problems that require creativity, we often reach a dead end without realizing it. We find ourselves circling around the same ineffective ideas and don't recognize when it's time to move on. In contrast, regularly switching back and forth between two tasks at a set interval can reset your thinking, enabling you to approach each task from fresh angles.

The Research

In an experiment, we randomly assigned participants to one of the preceding three approaches. The participants who were instructed to continually switch back and forth between two problems at a fixed interval were significantly more likely to find the correct answer to both problems than were participants who switched at their own discretion or halfway through the allotted time.

A second study focused on creative ideation. In this experiment, the problems we posed had no right answers. We wanted to find out whether the benefits of stepping away from a problem at regular intervals transferred to other types of problems warranting creativity, such as brainstorming.

Again, we randomly assigned participants to one of our three task-switching approaches and asked them to generate creative ideas for two tasks. As in the first study, most people believed that they would perform best if they switched between the two idea generation tasks at their own discretion. We again found that participants who were instructed to switch back and forth between the two tasks at a fixed interval came up with the most novel set of ideas.

The issue with both other approaches seemed to be that people failed to recognize when rigid thinking crept in. Participants who didn't step away from a task at regular intervals were more likely to write "new" ideas that were very similar to the last one they had written. While they might have felt that they were on a roll, the reality was that, without the breaks afforded by continual task switching, their actual progress was limited.

The creative benefits of switching tasks have been supported by other research. For example, Steven Smith of Texas A&M University and his colleagues found that individuals instructed to list items from different categories while continually switching back and forth between the categories generated more-novel ideas than did individuals who wrote down items from one category before switching to items from the other. In a similar vein, other studies have found that brief breaks during idea generation can increase the variety of ideas that people come up with. These researchers' findings, coupled with ours, suggest that the hustle and bustle of your daily work life may facilitate your creativity if it leads you to step away from a task and refresh your thinking.

How to Schedule Your Breaks

When you're working on tasks that would benefit from creative thinking, consciously insert breaks to refresh your approach. Set them at regular intervals—use a timer if you have to. When it goes off, switch tasks: Organize your reimbursement receipts, check your email, or clean your desk, and then return to the original task. If you're hesitant to break away, because you feel that you're on a roll, be mindful that this feeling might be a false impression. We tend to generate redundant ideas when we don't take regular breaks; ask yourself whether your latest ideas are qualitatively different. Finally, don't skip your lunch breaks, and don't feel guilty about taking breaks, especially when you are feeling stuck. Doing so may actually be the best use of your time.

Jackson G. Lu is an associate professor at the Massachusetts Institute of Technology Sloan School of Management. Modupe Akinola is the Barbara and David

Zalaznick Professor of Business at Columbia Business School. She examines how stress affects individual and collective performance outcomes and explores the psychological, physiological, and organizational forces that reduce inclusiveness and inhibit the success of all employees, particularly underrepresented groups, in organizations. **Malia Mason** is the Courtney C. Brown Professor of Business at Columbia Business School. She was a postdoctoral fellow in cognitive neuroscience at Harvard Medical School.

CHAPTER 5

Get Your Brain Unstuck

by Ron Friedman

Your colleagues logged off hours ago, but you're still staring at the screen, waiting for a breakthrough. You haven't produced anything substantive for hours. Yet for reasons you can't understand, it's been impossible to walk away. Even now, the answer seems *so close*.

If your work involves creative thinking, you are bound to encounter times like this—times when you feel stuck. Perhaps you're not sure how to start a project, respond to a client email, or structure an upcoming presentation. You're trying to be productive, yet as you turn the problem over in your head again and again, you find yourself running into the same barriers.

Adapted from content posted on hbr.org, July 9, 2014 (product #H00WFV).

When this happens, a common reaction is to redouble your efforts. Who doesn't love a good persistence story? Most of us have been taught that the only thing standing between us and a successful outcome is hard work.

But the research tells us something different. While grit does have its role, when it comes to creative solutions, dogged persistence can actually backfire.

A funny thing happens when you're thinking about a problem. The more time you spend deliberating, the more your focus narrows.

It's an experience familiar to all of us. When you first encounter a problem, certain solutions immediately burst to the fore. Occasionally, none of them seem quite right, so you try to reexamine the issue, giving it a fresh look and then another. Before you know it, something counterproductive happens. You lose sight of the big picture and become fixated on details. And the harder you try, the less likely it is that unexpected, novel ideas will enter your train of thought. At this point, you've reached a point of diminishing returns on your efforts.

So what should you do?

Research suggests that when you find yourself at an impasse, it's often fruitful to use *psychological distance* as a tool. By temporarily directing your attention away from a problem, you allow your focus to dissipate, releasing its mental grip. When you let go, loose connections will suddenly appear, making creative insights more likely.

While most of us intuitively know that a three-day weekend or an extended vacation can yield a renewed perspective, those options aren't always available, especially when we're facing a deadline.

But that doesn't mean that we can't reap the benefits of psychological distance in our day-to-day work. Here are three practices that can help.

Struggling for more than 15 minutes? Switch tasks

Task-switching can be perilous. When we're making good progress, allowing distractions to hijack our attention can derail our focus. But the moment we experience ourselves getting stuck, the rules shift. Here, a well-timed distraction can be a boon to creativity.

When we let go of a problem, our perspective expands. This phenomenon explains why we discover so many solutions in odd places, like the shower, the commute back home, or the visit to the gym. Redirecting our attention to an unrelated task also provides room for incubation, a term psychologists use to describe nonconscious thinking. Studies show that after a brief distraction, people generate a greater number of creative solutions to a problem than do people who spend the same period focusing on it intently.

The trick is to recognize when you are feeling stuck and resist the temptation to power through. In many cases, it is precisely when we are at our most discouraged that we can derive the greatest benefit from walking away.

For tasks requiring creative thinking, schedule multiple sessions over several days

Often, the most productive way of resolving a difficult problem is to alternate between thinking about it very deeply and then strategically shifting your attention elsewhere. Instead of setting aside one continuous block of time to work on a creative project, schedule shorter, more frequent sessions. By planning multiple periods of deep thinking, you're guaranteed a few transitions away from your task, ensuring that your focus expands.

Put mind-wandering periods to good use

Creative solutions rarely emerge when we're in the office. Which is why it can be helpful to keep an ongoing list of "thinking problems" that you can access on the go. Glance at your list just before entering mind-wandering periods, like when you're going out for a sandwich or traveling between meetings. A new context can lead to a fresh perspective.

Ultimately, the key to harnessing the power of psychological distance involves accepting that often, the best ideas don't appear when we're pushing ourselves to work harder. They prefer sneaking up on us, the moment we look away.

———————

Ron Friedman is an award-winning psychologist and the founder of ignite80, a learning and development company that teaches leaders science-based strategies for building high-performing teams. His books include *The Best Place to Work: The Art and Science of Creating an Extraordinary Workplace* and, more recently, *Decoding Greatness: How the Best in the World Reverse Engineer Success.*

CHAPTER 6

Four Ways to Spark Creativity When You're Feeling Stressed

by Susan Peppercorn and Maren Gube

The human brain comes equipped with powerful response mechanisms to protect us during uncertain times. In disruptive or unpredictable situations, the brain tries to interpret incoming stimuli and form a plan of action if the news is bad. When precarious circumstances are prolonged and combined with anxiety and

---

Adapted from content posted on hbr.org, October 1, 2021 (product #H06LV1).

fear, the brain's biological response is to hide rather than explore. From an evolutionary point of view, survival ends up taking precedence over creativity, as the stress hormones that ready us for battle also interrupt the networks involved in creativity.

The cognitive load from this subconscious scanning and scenario-building is one reason that we may feel tired and uninspired—and less creative—when going through a stressful time (or living in a stressful time). Why is an awareness of these effects important? By understanding how the brain functions when we're under threat or dealing with potentially frightening challenges, we find it easier to design strategies to alleviate both the conscious and unconscious fears that arise in the face of disruption, thereby supporting our own creativity. Here are four strategies that incorporate this understanding of your brain's functionality to nourish and feed your creative instincts.

Reasserting Control

Experiencing a loss of control is one of the main symptoms of uncertainty and ambiguity. Continued uncertainty can provoke feelings of being adrift and make it hard to plan or make decisions. Under these conditions, your brain's emotional amygdala circuits become increasingly active: Instead of choosing proactive and thoughtful actions through the prefrontal cortex, you may become reactive and more likely to allow fear to guide you. Fear is the enemy of creative thinking because it directs neural resources toward neutralizing the perceived threat.

That's why it can be a good idea to reduce uncertainty by planning your own disruptions. "When we're the disruptors, it's still scary," says Jonathan Fields, host of the *Good Life Project* podcast. "But we have a sense of agency and a powerful connection to a reason. We don't know how it will end or if we'll be able to do what we set out to do, but at least we've chosen the direction, and we're heading toward our ultimate destination." According to Fields, this approach can center you enough so that you can maintain a sense of control, breathe more easily, and think more clearly. You feel these benefits because focusing on your own ultimate destination engages your prefrontal cortex, which, as the seat of planning and control, helps regulate your thoughts and emotions—and ultimately the behaviors that can lead you to either open or close your creative spigots.

Designing a Conducive Environment

Having clarity, direction, and the right mental tools reduces stress and fear of the unknown while giving the brain freedom to make creative connections rather than dealing with imminent threats. Yet remote and hybrid work have complicated that picture, making it more important to be intentional about how work, communication, and collaboration opportunities are structured. Without the chance office conversations that sometimes spark creativity, companies that care about product innovation need a way for their people to stay consistently creative, even at a distance.

Andrew Yanofsky, head of operations at toy manufacturer WowWee, explains how hybrid and remote work has forced teams to be more thoughtful and structured about the yields expected from brainstorming meetings. His company has made changes to reflect that reality. "Since we can't rely on face-to-face conversations for ideation," he says, "we have become more intentional about setting mandates for meetings, moderating the sessions, and monitoring the steps post-brainstorm. Someone is designated as the 'pen holder' for the whole process and keeps an eye on key deliverables from beginning to end." Although many people view creativity as a free form of outside-the-box thinking, Yanofsky explains that by "making a sandbox and then playing in it," his teams have formalized that process while ensuring that they provide psychological safety for contributors.

Exercising New Mental Muscles

As described, you're keeping the prefrontal cortex engaged and your fear at bay by taking ownership of your own disruption and clarifying how you and your teams approach creative processes. You can further step up creativity during stressful periods by cross-training your brain and immersing yourself in new and different activities. Research has shown that venturing outside your primary area of expertise can enhance creative thinking.

For example, one study revealed that diversifying your areas of focus can boost cognitive flexibility, which allows for more fluid ideation and creativity. Social media marketing consultant and composer Marie Incontrera chose this route and credits collaborating with Dorie Clark, an HBR contributor and one of Thinkers50's top business thinkers, as vital to sparking her creativity in a different direction from her core work. During the pandemic, Incontrera and Clark created a new work of musical theater, a lesbian spy musical called *Absolute Zero*, which was incubated in a prestigious development program run by Apples and Oranges Arts. Their goal is to bring the show to Broadway in five years.

Increasing Connection

Both individuals and organizations struggle with the creativity-killing effects of prolonged stress, disruption, and uncertainty. One solution to help our brain overcome these challenges is to facilitate the release of the "social hormone," oxytocin, in our brains. Lourdes Olvera-Marshall, a diversity and inclusion strategist and an executive coach, told us that her team works toward this by allowing time at the beginning of a Zoom meeting for non-task-related conversation so that colleagues can connect in a personal way. She also continues to make time to connect one-on-one with her team members at least every other week with no agenda. "I've seen how these small moments generate connection and psychological safety as team members feel more comfortable with each other," Olvera-Marshall explains. "Plus, the meetings are more fun."

This type of social connection becomes a powerful creativity booster in part because it increases mutual trust, a foundational element for creativity. Olvera-Marshall has seen a significant increase in idea sharing when a few meetings a week start with positive, personal interactions. "Everyone approaches work more relaxed, which activates the parasympathetic system and generates the right climate for new, diverse ideas, which in turn boosts motivation and creativity," she says.

By employing these strategies, Olvera-Marshall is helping her company's leaders foster not just individual creativity but also team creativity through socioemotional support. This approach improves the brain's neurochemical balance by reducing stress hormones and increasing pro-social hormones, helping to reconnect the creativity networks that continuous uncertainty may have disrupted.

With each of the proactive steps just described, you can turn the stress of disruption into fuel for creativity, lessening your evolutionary fear reflexes and instead nourishing and revitalizing your creative brain circuits. Implement these ideas any time your innovative juices need a boost but particularly during your toughest challenges. After all, periods of rapid change, disruption, and global uncertainty are arguably the times when bold, brave creativity is needed the most.

Susan Peppercorn is an executive career transition coach and speaker. She is the author of *Ditch Your Inner Critic at Work: Evidence-Based Strategies to Thrive in Your Career.* Numerous publications, including the *New York Times*, the *Wall Street Journal*, *Fast Company*, the *Boston Globe*, and *Self* magazine, have tapped her for career advice. **Maren Gube** is Executive Director of Resiliti. She guides organizations pursuing cultures of fearless collaborative creativity through her research and professional practice. Her award-winning work on creativity and why women leave STEM fields has earned citations on both sides of the Atlantic.

CHAPTER 7

You Know How to Focus—Learn How to Unfocus

by Srini Pillay

The ability to focus is an important driver of excellence. Focused techniques such as to-do lists, timetables, and calendar reminders help people to stay on task. Few would argue with that, and even if they did, there is evidence to support the idea that resisting distraction and staying present have benefits: Practicing mindfulness for 10 minutes a day, for example, can enhance leadership effectiveness by helping you become more able to regulate your emotions and make sense of past experiences.

Adapted from "Your Brain Can Only Take So Much Focus" on hbr.org, May 12, 2017 (product #H03NKH).

Yet as helpful as focus can be, there's also a downside to focus as it is commonly viewed.

The problem is that excessive focus exhausts the focus circuits in your brain. It can drain your energy and make you lose self-control. This energy drain can also make you more impulsive and less helpful. As a result, decisions are poorly thought-out, and you become less collaborative.

So what do we do then? Focus or unfocus?

In keeping with recent research, both focus and unfocus are vital. The brain operates optimally when it toggles between focus and unfocus, allowing you to develop resilience, enhance creativity, and make better decisions.

When you unfocus, you engage a brain circuit called the *default mode network*. Abbreviated as DMN, we used to think of it as the "do mostly nothing" circuit because it only came on when you stopped focusing effortfully. Yet, even when the mind is "at rest," this circuit uses 20% of the body's energy.

The DMN needs this energy because it is doing anything but resting. Under the brain's conscious radar, this circuit activates old memories; goes back and forth between the past, present, and future; and recombines different ideas. Using this new and previously inaccessible data, you develop enhanced self-awareness and a sense of personal relevance. And you can imagine creative solutions or predict the future, thereby leading to better decision-making too. The network also helps you tune into other people's thinking, thereby improving team understanding and cohesion.

RUN AN ENERGIZER TO SPARK A NEW IDEA

by Duncan Wardle

What are you doing when you get your best ideas? Showering? Jogging? Commuting? I've worked with thousands of individuals around the world, and I've never heard anyone say "working."

How do you get into that relaxed brain state on demand? By running an *energizer*: a quick exercise that can get you and your team members (or classmates or friends) to laugh and relax. This practice frees your brain up from tiresome executive functions like weekly meetings and reports and gives you access to your own unrelated knowledge and experience that can uncover new ideas.

Energizers come in all shapes and sizes. "Storyteller" is one example. Participants pretend they're the expert of some unique field (think a leading designer of parachutes for elephants) and are interviewed by other subjects in the room on their "expertise." Another example is "Heroes and Villains." In this exercise, a group is split into two teams, and each is asked to give a pitch for (heroes) or against (villains) a particular idea, such as hosting a Pet Olympics.

Of course, listening to a fictitious expert on elephant parachutes or adults debating a Pet Olympics invariably leads to laughter, and I've found that playfulness (in the form of laughter) triggers relaxation. In this state, the parts of your brain that allow a stray

(continued)

RUN AN ENERGIZER TO SPARK A NEW IDEA

thought, a random memory, or an image to surface can combine in novel ways.

Although it would be unfeasible to be this playful all the time, energizers are a great way to bring in structured moments of play during team meetings, in the classroom, or just in your daily life as a way to unlock the parts of your brain that sit idle throughout the day.

Duncan Wardle is the former vice president of innovation and creativity at the Walt Disney Company. He launched his creative consulting company iD8 & innov8 to help companies embed a culture of innovation and creativity across their entire organization.

Adapted from "So, You Think You're Not Creative," Ascend, on hbr.org, March 29, 2021.

There are many simple and effective ways to activate this circuit in the course of a day.

Use positive constructive daydreaming

Positive constructive daydreaming (PCD) is a type of mind-wandering different from slipping into a daydream or guiltily rehashing worries. When you build this practice into your day deliberately, it can boost your creativity, strengthen your leadership ability, and reenergize the brain. To start PCD, you choose a low-key activity such as knitting, gardening, or casual reading, then wander into the recesses of your mind. But unlike slipping into a daydream or guilty, dysphoric daydreaming, you might first imagine something playful and wishful—like running through the woods or lying on a yacht. Then you swivel your attention from the external world to the internal, with this image in mind while still doing the low-key activity.

Studied for decades by psychology professor Jerome Singer, PCD activates the default mode network and metaphorically changes the silverware that your brain uses to find information. While focused attention is like a fork—picking up obvious conscious thoughts that you have—PCD commissions a different set of silverware. It employs a spoon for scooping up the delicious mélange of flavors of your identity (the scent of your grandmother, the feeling of satisfaction with the first bite of apple pie on a crisp fall day) and chopsticks for connecting ideas across your brain (to enhance innovation). PCD also uses a marrow spoon for getting into the nooks and crannies of your brain to pick up long-lost memories that are a vital part of your identity. In this state, your sense of self is enhanced—which, according to business scholar Warren Bennis, is the essence of leadership. This sense of self is your psychological center of gravity, a grounding mechanism that helps you boost your agility and manage change more effectively too.

Take a nap

In addition to building in time for PCD, leaders can also consider authorized napping. Not all naps are the same.

When your brain is in a slump, your clarity and creativity are compromised. Studies show that after a 10-minute nap, you become much clearer and more alert. But if you have a creative task in front of you, you will probably need a full 90 minutes for more complete brain refreshing. Your brain requires this longer time to make more associations and dredge up ideas that lie in the recesses of your memory network.

Pretend to be someone else

When you're stuck in a creative process, unfocus may also come to the rescue when you embody and live out an entirely different personality. Educational psychologists Denis Dumas and Kevin Dunbar found that people who try to solve creative problems are more successful if they behave like an eccentric poet rather than a rigid librarian. Given a test in which they have to come up with as many uses as possible for any object (for example, a brick), those who behave like eccentric poets have superior creative performance. This finding holds even if the same person takes on a different identity.

When in a creative deadlock, try this exercise of embodying a different identity. This exercise is likely to get you out of your own head, and it allows you to think from another person's perspective. I call this practice *psychological halloweenism.*

For years, focus has been the venerated ability among all abilities. Since we spend 46.9% of our days with our minds wandering away from a task at hand, we crave the ability to keep it fixed and on task. Yet if we built PCD, 10- and 90-minute naps, and psychological halloween-ism into our days, we would probably preserve focus for when we need it, and we'd use it much more efficiently too. More importantly, the ability to unfocus will allow us to update information in our brains, giving us access to deeper parts of ourselves and enhancing our agility, creativity, and decision-making.

Srini Pillay, MD, is the cofounder of Reulay and the CEO of NeuroBusiness Group. He is also a technology innovator and entrepreneur in the health and leadership development sectors and an award-winning author. His latest book is *Tinker, Dabble, Doodle, Try: Unlock the Power of the Unfocused Mind*. He was formerly a part-time assistant professor at Harvard Medical School and has taught in the Executive Education Programs at Harvard Business School and Duke Corporate Education.

CHAPTER 8

Look Outside Your Industry for More-Creative Solutions

by Bill Taylor

A big challenge in times of disruption and uncertainty is for people and organizations to keep learning as fast as the world is changing—to analyze problems they haven't encountered before and to make sense of opportunities they haven't thought about before.

That's why leaders should encourage their colleagues to learn from experts in fields they've never worked in.

Adapted from "To Find Creative Solutions, Look Outside Your Industry" on hbr.org, February 7, 2022 (product #H06UUV).

Practices that are routine in one industry can be revolutionary when they migrate to another, especially when they challenge conventional wisdom in that industry. What better way to fuel your company's imagination than to look for inspiration outside your field? If you want to learn fast, learn from strangers.

In their book *Benchmarking for Best Practices*, Christopher E. Bogan and Michael J. English share a business case study that illustrates how accepted ideas from one field can quickly transform another field. "In 1912," they write, "a curious Henry Ford watched men cut meat during a tour of a Chicago slaughterhouse. The carcasses were hanging on hooks mounted on a monorail. After each man performed his job, he would push the carcass to the next station. When the tour was over, the tour guide said, 'Well, sir, what do you think?' Mr. Ford turned to the man and said, 'Thanks, son, I think you may have given me a real good idea.' Less than six months later, the world's first assembly line started producing magnetos in the Ford Highland Park Plant."

Or consider a more timely case study: A *Wall Street Journal* article by Ben Kesling described how the chaplain of an overwhelmed hospital in Chicago helped nurses deal with the mental and emotional fallout of the early Covid-19 wave and the rise of the Omicron variant. This chaplain, who was also an army veteran, "noticed that phrases nurses were using in conversation sounded like what he had heard from troops who had served in combat zones." So, to help nurses stay strong as they waged war on the virus, he borrowed concepts and techniques developed by the army to help troops deal with the trauma of war. "He could actually draw that parallel between us and people that have been veterans of war," one nurse marveled about the chaplain and his program. "I never even made that connection because for me—I've been a nurse for 20 years on this unit—I've never seen this kind of trauma to our team ever. So when he made that connection, I was like, oh my gosh, how have I never realized that?"

Take another example: Several years ago, London's Great Ormond Street Hospital, a children's hospital renowned for its cardiac care, was struggling with poorly designed handoffs when it transferred patients from one step of a complex medical procedure to the next. So Martin Elliott, head of cardiac surgery, and Allan Goldman, head of pediatric intensive care, studied high-powered professionals who, despite being from a totally unrelated field, were better than anyone else was at organizing handoffs—the pit crew of Ferrari's Formula One racing team.

The doctors and the pit crew worked together at the team's racing center in Italy, at the British Grand Prix, and in the hospital's operating room. Members of the pit crew were struck by how clumsy the hospital's handoff process was, not to mention the fact that it often lacked a clear leader. (In Formula One races, a so-called lollipop man wields an easy-to-see paddle and calls the shots.) Moreover, they noted how noisy the process was. Ferrari pit crews operate largely in silence, despite (or because of) the roar of engines around them. Thanks to the techniques the medical staff learned from these outsiders—techniques that were accepted wisdom in

racing circles—the hospital redesigned its handoff procedures and sharply reduced medical errors.

Learning from strangers doesn't always have to be
about dealing with an unfamiliar situation or solving a
specific problem. Colonel Dean Esserman, during his
transformational tenure as chief of police in Providence,
Rhode Island, pushed his insular department to open
itself up to original ideas, and new ways of thinking.
One of his initiatives was a fabulously creative program
called Cops and Docs. Esserman's detectives regularly
sat in with doctors at Brown University Medical School
as the physicians discussed tough cases. The detectives
watched and listened as the doctors analyzed clues about
a patient (symptoms), sorted through evidence (test results), and identified the culprit (disease).

In turn, doctors sat in on the police department's
command meeting to learn how cops dealt with conflicting and confusing information, ruled out suspects, and
cracked their cases. Esserman's goal was for his department to "become a place that embraces research, that
figures out and spreads methodologies that work in ways
that medical schools do." For set-in-their-ways detectives
to learn new perspectives on policing, their chief understood they had to learn from experts in a field unrelated
to policing.

These times of rapid change and instability have created all kinds of questions for leaders and organizations.
One of the biggest questions is this: Do we have new
ideas about where to look for new ideas? When it comes
to innovation and problem-solving, there will always

be a place for old-fashioned, time-consuming R&D—research and development.

Today, though, there is also a place for a different kind of R&D—rip off and duplicate. The fastest way for organizations to make sense of challenges they are seeing for the first time is to survey unrelated fields for ideas that have been working for a long time. Why gamble on untested strategies and insights if you can quickly apply strategies and insights that are already proven elsewhere? That's how leaders can help their colleagues keep learning as fast as the world is changing.

Bill Taylor is the cofounder of *Fast Company* and the author, most recently, of *Simply Brilliant: How Great Organizations Do Ordinary Things in Extraordinary Ways*. Learn more at williamctaylor.com.

Brainstorming and Beyond

CHAPTER 9

Better Brainstorming

by Hal Gregersen

About 20 years ago, I was leading a brainstorming session in one of my MBA classes, and it was like wading through oatmeal. We were talking about something that many organizations struggle with: how to build a culture of equality in a male-dominated environment. Though it was an issue the students cared about, they clearly felt uninspired by the ideas they were generating. After a lot of discussion, the energy level in the room was approaching nil. Glancing at the clock, I resolved to at least give us a starting point for the next session.

"Everyone," I improvised, "let's forget about finding answers for today and just come up with some new

Adapted from an article in *Harvard Business Review*, March–April 2018 (product #R1802C).

questions we could be asking about this problem. Let's see how many we can write down in the time we have left." The students dutifully started to throw out questions, and I scribbled them on a chalkboard, redirecting anybody who started to suggest an answer. To my surprise, the room was quickly energized. At the end of the session, people left talking excitedly about a few of the questions that had emerged—those that challenged basic assumptions we had been making. For instance, were there grassroots efforts we could support rather than rules that we would hand down from the top? And instead of automatically looking elsewhere for best practices, what could we learn from pockets within our own organization that had achieved equality? Suddenly, there was much more to discuss, because we had opened up unexpected pathways to potential solutions.

Brainstorming for questions, not answers, wasn't something I'd tried before. It just occurred to me in that moment, probably because I had recently been reading sociologist Parker Palmer's early work about creative discovery through open, honest inquiry. But this technique worked so well with the students that I began experimenting with it in consulting engagements, and eventually it evolved into a methodology that I continue to refine. By now I've used it with hundreds of clients, including global teams at Chanel, Danone, Disney, EY, Fidelity, Genentech, Salesforce, and dozens of other companies; nonprofit organizations; and individual leaders I've coached.

Underlying the approach is a broader recognition that fresh questions often beget novel—even transformative—insights. Consider this example from the field of psychology: Before 1998, virtually all well-trained psychologists focused on attacking the roots of mental disorders and deficits, on the assumption that well-being came down to the absence of those negative conditions. But then Martin Seligman became president of the American Psychological Association, and he reframed things for his colleagues. What if, he asked in a speech at the APA's annual meeting, well-being is just as driven by the *presence* of certain *positive* conditions—keys to flourishing that could be recognized, measured, and cultivated? With that question, the positive psychology movement was born.

Brainstorming for questions rather than answers makes it easier to push past cognitive biases and venture into uncharted territory. We've seen this dynamic in academic studies—in social psychologist Adam Galinsky's research on the power of reframing during times of transition, for instance. Yet lingering in a questioning mode doesn't come naturally to most people, because we're conditioned from an early age to just keep the answers coming.

The methodology I've developed is essentially a process for recasting problems in valuable new ways. It helps people adopt a more creative habit of thinking and, when they're looking for breakthroughs, gives them a sense of control. There's actually something they can do other than sit and wait for a bolt from the blue. Here, I'll describe how and why this approach works. You can use it anytime you (in a group or individually) are feeling stuck or trying to imagine new possibilities. And if you make it a regular practice in your organization, this type of brainstorming can foster a stronger culture of collective problem-solving and truth-seeking.

What Process Should We Follow?

Over the years, I have tested variations of this brainstorming process—I now call it a *question burst*—and collected and analyzed participant data and feedback to gauge what works best. I've experimented with different group sizes, time allotments, and numbers of questions; impromptu versus scheduled sessions; various modes of capturing ideas; and greater and lesser amounts of coaching (on, for example, what constitutes a good question and how to make creative leaps in thinking). I've done temperature checks in sessions and conducted surveys after them, looking for the effects of each variation. Over time the question burst has settled into a standard format, which consists of three steps.

1. Set the stage

To begin, select a challenge you care deeply about. Perhaps you've suffered a setback or you have a vague sense of an intriguing opportunity. How do you know it's ripe for a breakthrough question? It's probably a good candidate if it "makes your heart beat fast," as Intuit's former chair and CEO, Brad Smith, put it to me. You'll give it your full attention and want to engage others in thinking about it.

Invite a few people to help you consider that challenge from fresh angles. Though you can do this exercise on your own, bringing others into the process will give you access to a wider knowledge base and help you maintain a constructive mindset. As Ned Hallowell says in his book *Driven to Distraction at Work* (which was based on his decades of research on how to sustain productive attention), worry "feasts on a solitary victim." When you ask others to participate in a question burst, you're making yourself vulnerable by sharing the problem—but you're also summoning empathy, which fosters idea generation, as we've learned from design thinking. And you engage others in the cause in a nonthreatening way.

It's best to include two or three people who have no direct experience with the problem and whose cognitive style or worldview is starkly different from yours. They will come up with surprising, compelling questions that you would not, because they have no practiced ways of thinking about the problem and no investment in the status quo. They're more likely to ask third-rail questions and point to elephants in the room—they don't know not to.

In traditional brainstorming—the kind that focuses on generating answers—individuals perform better than groups, on average. That's because powerful group dynamics such as social loafing (coasting on others' contributions) and social anxiety (fears about how your ideas will be judged) can hinder original thinking and stifle the voices of introverted members. But the question-burst methodology, by design, reverses many of those destructive dynamics by prompting people to depart from their usual habits of social interaction. For one thing, it creates a safe space for anyone, including a quieter person, to offer a different perspective. Because a question burst doesn't demand that anyone instantly assert a point of view, people often feel more comfortable speaking up. The sole focus on questions also suspends the automatic rush to provide an answer—and ultimately helps expand the problem space for deeper exploration.

Once you've gathered your partners for this exercise, give yourself just two minutes to lay out the problem for them. People often believe that their problems require detailed explanations. But quickly sharing the challenge forces you to frame it in a high-level way that doesn't constrain or direct the questioning. So just hit the highlights. Try to convey how things would change for the better if the problem were solved. And briefly say why you are stuck—why it hasn't already been solved.

This approach helped Odessa, a manager at a global financial services company, reframe what she initially viewed as a complex communications challenge: rolling out a new strategy to people performing different tasks at many levels across many geographic locations. She prefaced her question burst with a simple explanation, sharing her hopes for getting everyone "rowing in the same direction" and her frustration that one set of messages couldn't do the job, given employees' diverse roles and perspectives. With this simple explanation, she created room for a line of questioning that radically altered her understanding. She came to see the problem as a leadership challenge, not just an internal marketing campaign. If she could find a way to trust others to convey the strategy, she could mobilize a small army of managers in the field to tailor messages for maximum local impact.

NOT ALL QUESTIONS ARE CREATED EQUAL

Often, as I'm outlining the rules for a question burst, people ask what kinds of questions they should contribute—or how they can be confident that a question is a good one for further pursuit. While I hesitate to be definitive about this, not all questions have equal potential to lead to novel solutions. To up your odds, keep these principles in mind:

- Traditional divergent-thinking techniques (for example, making random associations or taking on an alternative persona) can help unlock new questions and, ultimately, new territory.

- Questions are most productive when they are open versus closed, short versus long, and simple versus complex.

- Descriptive questions (What's working? What's not? Why?) work best if they precede speculative ones (What if? What might be? Why not?).

- Complex questions that demand creative synthesis produce better breakthrough thinking than simple questions that require only recall.

- Questions are annoying and distracting when they don't spring from a deeply held conviction about what the group wants to achieve.

- Questions are toxic when they are posed aggressively, put people on the spot, cast unwarranted doubt on their ideas, or cultivate a culture of fear.

Before opening the floor to your group, clearly spell out two critical rules: First, people can contribute only questions. Those who try to suggest solutions—or respond to others' questions—will be redirected by you, the convener of the session. And second, no preambles or justifications that frame a question will be allowed, because they'll guide listeners to see the problem in a certain way—the very thing you're trying to avoid.

You'll also want to do a quick emotion check up front. As the owner of the challenge, take a moment to reflect on it: Are your feelings about it positive, neutral, or negative? Jot down a few words that capture your own baseline mood. No need to spend more than 10 seconds on this. You'll do the same thing again after the session is over. These checks are important because emotions affect creative energy. The exercise's objective is not only to spark valuable new questions but also to provide an emotional boost that will make you more likely to follow up on them.

Here I should point out that your creative energy will ebb and flow in the coming days, weeks, and months—and preparing yourself for that is critical. Transformational ideas start out as exhilarating but turn vexing as unforeseen snags reveal themselves. Then they settle into hard work that, with luck, produces moments of hope that will see the change through. If you expect this turbulence from the beginning, you'll be better able to ride it out later.

2. Brainstorm the questions

Now set a timer and spend the next four minutes collectively generating as many questions as possible about the challenge. As in all brainstorming, don't allow pushback on anyone's contributions. The more surprising and pro-vocative the questions, the better.

When working with large enterprises, I often notice that senior leaders in particular find it excruciatingly dif-ficult to resist offering answers—even for four minutes—when people start throwing out questions. At one manu-facturing company, for instance, when questions about supply chain issues started bubbling up, the group's leader couldn't help jumping in to display his knowl-edge. This impulse is understandable, and not just for senior executives. In a hierarchy, any manager's failure to have ready answers may be perceived as an embarrass-ing stumble. Questions, especially counterintuitive ones, make many of us feel so uncomfortable that we hasten to utter any default response that buys us time to recover. But when we're feeling blocked on a problem, answering questions this way is a waste of time. After all, the reason we're hung up is that our go-to answers aren't getting us anywhere.

In this exercise, the emphasis is on quantity. By ask-ing the group to generate as many questions as possible in the time allotted—try for at least 15 questions—you'll keep them short, simple, and fresh. Write every question down verbatim on paper or type it into a laptop or a tab-let instead of using a whiteboard. This way, you can cap-ture everything accurately. And ask group members to keep you honest afterward. Otherwise you might com-mit unconscious censoring that repels lines of inquiry you don't immediately understand or want to hear.

As you're recording, add your own questions to the mix. Doing so will often reveal patterns in how you have habitually framed a problem (and might have unknowingly perpetuated it).

Is there some magic about precisely four minutes and 15 questions? No, but the time pressure helps participants stick to the questions-only rule. Any effort spent on answers will mean less chance of hitting the goal. People will also be more likely to generate questions that are unburdened by qualifications and assumptions, and they'll find it easier to resist explaining why they're asking a question that might seem to come from left field. Even better, studies show that moderate performance pressures can enhance creative output.

Moreover, perhaps because selective, sustained attention places real demands on the human brain, energy often wanes in this exercise after three and a half minutes, especially for beginners. And as a practical matter, transcribing dozens of questions can turn into an onerous task. For both those reasons, it's better to use multiple question bursts to reshape, refine, and ultimately solve a challenge than to cram too much activity into one longer session.

Once the timer goes off, do a second quick emotional check. How do you feel about the challenge now? (And how do others in the group feel about it?) Are you more positive than you were four minutes ago? If not, and if the setting allows, maybe rerun the exercise. Or get some rest and try again tomorrow. Or try it with some different people. Research has established that creative problem solving flourishes when people work in positive emotional states. After poring over survey data from more than 1,500 global leaders, I'm convinced that part of the power of the question burst lies in its ability to alter a person's view of the challenge, by dislodging—for most—that feeling of being stuck.

3. Identify a quest—and commit to it

On your own, study the questions you jotted down, looking for those that suggest new pathways. About 80% of the time, this exercise produces at least one question that usefully reframes the problem and provides a new angle for solving it. Select a few questions that intrigue you, that strike you as different from how you've been going about things, or even that cause you to feel a bit uncomfortable.

Now try expanding those few into their own sets of related or follow-up questions. A classic way of doing this is the five-whys sequence developed by Toyota Industries' founder, Sakichi Toyoda—or its variation suggested by Stanford University's Michael Ray in his book *The Highest Goal*. Ask yourself why the question you chose seemed important or meaningful. Then ask why the reason you just gave is important—or why it's a sticking point. And so on. By better understanding why a question really matters and what obstacles you might face in addressing it, you deepen your resolve and ability to do something about it and further broaden the territory of possible solutions. In the case of Odessa, the manager with a strategy to roll out, one breakthrough question—Could you recruit field leaders to communicate it locally?—provoked other questions: Why haven't I done that in the past? Could I trust others to do this well? Why do I have a problem extending that trust?

Finally, commit to pursuing at least one new pathway you've glimpsed—and do so as a *truth seeker*. I steal that term from *The Right Kind of Crazy*, NASA engineer Adam Steltzner's account of working at the Jet Propulsion Laboratory, where freewheeling people manage to accomplish things like landing a robotic rover on Mars. Set aside considerations of what might be more comfortable to conclude or easier to implement, and instead adopt an innovator's focus on the "job to be done" and what it will take to get the problem solved. Devise a near-term action plan: What concrete actions will you personally take in the next three weeks to find potential solutions suggested by your new questions?

After one question burst I helped facilitate, a chief marketing officer from a multidivisional company resolved to track down some facts. He had been wrestling with concerns about hypercompetitive behaviors in his business unit. In a question-burst session he led with others, it dawned on him that he had been making a big assumption: that the founders of his division had chosen its unique compensation scheme to create a culture of internal rivalry. His to-do list started with getting on their calendars and asking them about this. Guess what? Not only was this not a culture they had aimed for, but they were dismayed to learn it existed. His meetings with them gave rise to a new emphasis on culture and values in the unit—and created the context in which the chief marketing officer could intervene and address toxic behaviors. The point here is that arriving at assumption-challenging questions is essential but never sufficient. An action plan and follow-up can clarify the problem and break open the pathway to change.

How Can We Make Question Bursts a Habit?

I usually recommend doing at least three rounds of the question-burst exercise for a given issue. Although it's valuable as a one-off activity, the more you do it, the deeper you'll go in your thinking. After the leader of a development team at a global software company did the exercise repeatedly, she came to the realization that her original conception of a problem was, in her words, "superficial." Through persistent questioning, she told me, she "arrived at a much more meaningful challenge to conquer."

Even with three rounds, the time investment is minimal. It's an efficient path to fresh perspectives and creativity. The process will also get easier the more you do it. When people crank up their questioning activity for the first time with this approach, it feels strange because it's out of line with established norms at work and in life. Since childhood, they've been conditioned not to ask questions.

James T. Dillon, an education professor emeritus at the University of California, Riverside, spent a career studying this phenomenon in classrooms. He was shocked by how rarely students asked questions—which are critical to learning. The problem wasn't a lack of curiosity. "Every time that conditions have been provided for them (not by a mere pause, 'Any questions? No? OK, open your books'), a flood of intriguing student questions has poured forth," Dillon writes in his book *Questioning and Teaching*. When he surveyed other teachers about this, they almost universally agreed that "students indeed have questions but do not go on to ask them in class." Why not? They're afraid to do so, Dillon says, "largely because of their experience with negative reactions from the teacher (and from classmates)." They learn to keep their questions to themselves and to repeat back well-rehearsed answers when quizzed by their teachers, according to Tony Wagner, a senior fellow at the Learning Policy Institute. Other researchers—looking at arenas of human learning and interaction such as community forums, medical consultations, political institutions, and workplaces—have consistently come to the same conclusion: Questioning is an innate human behavior that's actively subverted and systematically shut down.

And power struggles don't help matters. In social groups, dominant individuals inevitably emerge; left unchecked, they find ways to build and perpetuate their power. One common way to do this is to silence questioners—those pesky, curious minds whose queries might suggest that the leader hasn't quite figured it all out.

Of course, many business leaders, recognizing the imperative for constant innovation, do try to encourage questions. But their employees have already internalized the habit of not asking them—especially the tough ones. We need to change this habit. That's what my MIT colleague Robert Langer, the health-care technology innovator who has been called the "Edison of medicine," has been doing with his students and postdocs. In an interview he said, "When you're a student, you're judged by how well you answer questions. Somebody else asks the questions, and if you give good answers, you'll get a good grade. But in life, you're judged by how good your questions are." As he mentors people, he explicitly focuses their attention on making this all-important transition, knowing that "they'll become great professors, great entrepreneurs—great something—if they ask good questions."

Organizations can raise their questioning quotient in various ways. For example, in my field experience, I've found that people become better questioners in environments where they're encouraged to value creative friction in everyday work. At companies like Amazon, ASOS, IDEO, Patagonia, Pixar, Tesla, and Zappos, for example, people often come together to tackle challenges by asking one another tough questions—in hallways, lunchrooms, or even conference rooms. Research by management professors Andrew Hargadon of University of California, Davis, and Beth Bechky of New York University shows that those volunteering ideas in such companies do not mindlessly spit back answers to the questions posed. People respectfully build on the comments and actions of others, considering "not only the original question but also whether there is a better question to be asked." As they do this over and over, new solutions emerge.

People also become better questioners in organizational cultures where they feel safe doggedly pursuing the truth, no matter where it takes them. To create such cultures, MIT's Ed Schein says, leaders must show humility, vulnerability, and trust, and they must empower others and treat them equitably. When those conditions aren't present, questions tend to be constrained or, worse, crushed.

Interestingly, when I've facilitated question bursts with large groups (broken down into subgroups of three to six people), I have noticed that the people least likely to engage in the exercise and follow the rules are the folks with the highest positions or greatest technical expertise. Whether they feel they're above the exercise or worry that sharing problems will make them appear incompetent, they cripple the truth-seeking capability of the entire group as others watch them disengage or scoff at contributions. If that's the example and tone that leaders are setting in a single microcosmic exercise, imagine the dampening impact they have on inquiry throughout their organizations.

Finally, people must hold themselves accountable for follow-up. Few things are more annoying than a colleague who *only* asks questions. People must take responsibility for exploring the pathways those questions open up and discovering valuable answers. This is especially true for leaders. Everyone else is taking cues from them about when, where, how, and why the status quo should be challenged. Leaders must carve out time to help gather and analyze newer, better, and different information. It's a sign of ownership when leaders go out of their way to do that. It shows others that management is committed to crafting a future where questions count.

Hal Gregersen is Executive Director of the MIT Leadership Center, a Senior Lecturer in Leadership and Innovation at the MIT Sloan School of Management, a Thinkers50 globally ranked management thinker, and the founder of the 4-24 Project. He is also the author of *Questions Are the Answer: A Breakthrough Approach to Your Most Vexing Problems at Work and in Life* and a coauthor of *The Innovator's DNA: Mastering the Five Skills of Disruptive Innovators*.

CHAPTER 10

The Problem-Solving Process That Prevents Groupthink

by Art Markman

There are two reasons most of us aren't very good at creative problem-solving. First, few people get training in how to be creative. Second, few people understand group dynamics well enough to harness their own power to help groups maximize their creativity.

Resolving the first issue requires getting your employees to learn more about the way they think . . . a tall order

Adapted from content posted on hbr.org, November 25, 2015 (product #H02IBI).

for managers. The second issue, though, is well within your ability to change.

A key element of creativity is bringing existing knowledge to bear on a new problem or goal. The more people who can engage with that problem or goal, the more knowledge that is available to work on it. Unfortunately, much research demonstrates that the traditional brainstorming methods—first described by Alex Osborn in the 1950s—fail. When groups get together and simply start throwing out ideas, they actually come up with fewer ideas overall and fewer novel, actionable ideas than what the same individuals would have generated had they worked alone.

Managing Divergent and Convergent Thinking

To fix this problem, we need to think about the two phases of group problem-solving: *divergence* and *convergence.*

Divergence happens when the group considers as many different potential solutions as possible. For example, a common test of creativity is the alternative-uses exercise. People are to try to create as many unique uses as they can.

Convergence happens when multiple proposed solutions are evaluated. In this phase, a large set of ideas is whittled to a smaller set of candidate solutions to the current problem.

The core principle of group creativity is that individuals working alone diverge, whereas group members working together converge. In group settings, as soon as one person shares a potential solution with everyone else, this idea influences the memory of every person in the group in ways that make everyone think about the problem more similarly. That is why groups working together diverge less than do individuals working alone.

To generate ideas, diverge first.

To fix group idea generation, then, be aware of when you are trying to diverge and when you are trying to converge. For example, early in the process of problem-solving, think carefully about the problem itself. Have your group members work alone to craft statements describing the problem. Then, get them back together to discuss their descriptions. The individuals are likely to come up with a variety of distinct problem statements. The group discussion will lead everyone to accept one variant or a few variants of these statements to work on. This individual, then group approach creates healthy convergence.

To generate solutions, *also* diverge first.

When you start to generate solutions, you again want to begin with divergence. As you did for problem descriptions, have people work alone to start. Then collect these initial ideas, send them around to other group members, and allow the divergence to continue as group members individually build on the ideas of their colleagues. Because people are still working alone, the way they build on other people's ideas is still going to be different from how other group members are building on those ideas.

After this process, you can give the resulting ideas to everyone and then let the group get together to discuss them. This discussion will gradually lead the group to converge on a small number of candidate solutions.

This process maximizes the contribution of the group. Everyone gets to engage their knowledge in service of the problem to be solved without having their memories or opinions influenced by other people's solutions. Everyone is also able to enhance the ideas generated by their colleagues. Finally, the group gets to work together to build further on the ideas and to evaluate the candidates.

This simple procedure works effectively, because it respects what individuals and groups do best.

———————

Art Markman is the Annabel Irion Worsham Centennial Professor of Psychology and Marketing at the University of Texas at Austin and Founding Director of the program in the Human Dimensions of Organizations. He has written over 150 scholarly papers on numerous topics, including reasoning, decision-making, and motivation. His most recent book is *Bring Your Brain to Work: Using Cognitive Science to Get a Job, Do It Well, and Advance Your Career* (Harvard Business Review Press, 2019).

CHAPTER 11

A Smarter Way to Wrap Up Your Brainstorm

by Angus Fletcher

Almost every business, of every size, across sectors, employs creativity training, from whiteboard brainstorming sessions to design thinking. It's a billion-dollar industry. But there's a problem: The training doesn't work. Instead, it perpetuates expert bias and pseudo-innovation. And although it can temporarily boost morale, it does little over the long haul to reduce burnout. On the whole, research has shown creativity training to be at best inadequate and at worst counterproductive.[1]

Adapted from "3 Exercises to Boost Your Team's Creativity" on hbr.org, March 24, 2022 (product #H06XE3).

To understand what's broken and how to fix it, my lab partnered with teams at a variety of organizations, among them Silicon Valley startups, U.S. Special Operations, the University of Chicago Booth School of Business, and *Fortune* 50 companies. One of our key findings had to do with how you *finish* a brainstorm.

Most brainstorming sessions wrap up with the group's attempting to select the best ideas on the whiteboard. When you do that, you're actually attempting to eliminate the worst ideas through logical techniques such as convergent and critical thinking.

This wrap-up approach is counterproductive. It reinstates whatever biases you managed to escape during the brainstorm, and it kills your most promising creations. Because those creations, like newborns, will be less developed than the old standbys, they will often get crossed off the whiteboard as imperfect or impractical. What these nascent intuitions need instead is further development, via counterfactual thinking.

A more effective approach is to use this two-step, meet-the-moment process called *storythinking*.

For step 1, take each of your team's newly imagined options and rank it on the scale you see in figure 11-1. Options with a low ranking (0–2) are low in creativity and low in innovation potential. Options with a high ranking (8–10) are moderate-to-low in creativity but high in innovation potential. Options in the middle (3–7) are low-to-moderate in innovation potential but high in creativity.

For step 2, assess your current operational environment. Is it stable or volatile? Certain or uncertain? If it's

FIGURE 11-1

Creativity in the moment

As an alternative to brainstorming sessions for idea generation, use this two-step storythinking process to help identify and develop ideas.

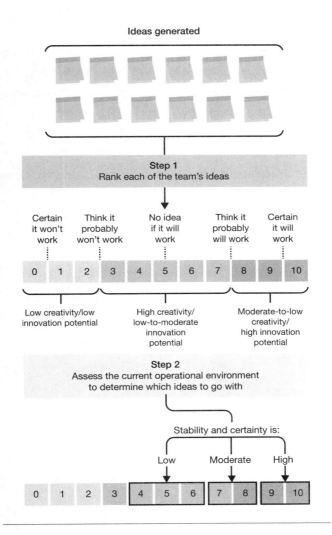

high in stability and certainty, go with an option ranked 9 or 10. If it's moderate, go with a 7 or 8. If it's low, go with a 4 or 6. (That's not a typo. Go with a 4, an option you think might not work.) If it has no stability or certainty, go with a 5.

In stable and certain environments, highly creative options are less likely to work, so there's no need to try them. In unstable and uncertain environments, less creative options are doomed, so the value proposition lies in gambling on a long shot. This method matches your originality to the moment.

———————————

Angus Fletcher is Professor of Story Science at Ohio State's Project Narrative. More of his research can be found at www.angusfletcher.co.

NOTE

1. Patrick J. Kiger, "Practice Does Not Necessarily Make Perfect When It Comes to Creativity," *Insights by Stanford Business*, September 10, 2020, www.gsb.stanford.edu/insights/practice-does-not -necessarily-make-perfect-when-it-comes-creativity.

CHAPTER 12

Find Innovation Where You Least Expect It

by Tony McCaffrey and Jim Pearson

On the evening of April 14, 1912, the RMS *Titanic* collided with an iceberg in the North Atlantic and sank two hours and 40 minutes later. Of its 2,200 passengers and crew, only 705 survived, plucked out of 16 lifeboats by the RMS *Carpathia*. Imagine how many more might have lived if crew members had thought of the iceberg as not just the cause of the disaster but a lifesaving solution. The iceberg rose high above the water and stretched some 400 feet in length. The lifeboats might have ferried

Adapted from an article in *Harvard Business Review*, December 2015 (product #R1512F).

people there to look for a flat spot. The *Titanic* itself was navigable for a while and might have been able to pull close enough to the iceberg for people to scramble onto it. Such a rescue operation was not without precedent: Some 60 years before, 127 of 176 passengers emigrating from Ireland to Canada saved themselves in the Gulf of St. Lawrence by climbing aboard an ice floe.

It's impossible to know if this rescue attempt would have worked. At the least it's an intriguing idea—yet surprisingly difficult to envision. If you were to ask a group of executives, even creative product managers and marketers, to come up with innovative scenarios in which all the *Titanic's* passengers could have been saved, they would very likely have the same blind spot that the crew had. The reason is a common psychological bias—called functional fixedness—that limits a person to seeing an object only in the way in which it is traditionally used. In a nautical context, an iceberg is a hazard to be avoided; it's very hard to see it any other way.

When it comes to innovation, businesses are constantly hampered by functional fixedness and other cognitive biases that cause people to overlook elegant solutions hidden in plain sight. We have spent years investigating how innovative designs can be built by harnessing the power of the commonly overlooked. We have identified techniques and tools to help you overcome cognitive traps and solve problems in innovative ways—whether you are conceiving new products, finding novel applications for existing products, or anticipating competitive threats. Using the tools doesn't require special talents or heroic degrees of creativity; taken together, they form a simple, low-cost, systematic way to spur innovation.

To understand how the tools work, let's first look at the three cognitive barriers they address.

Functional Fixedness

In the 1930s, German psychologist Karl Duncker demonstrated the phenomenon of functional fixedness with a famous brainteaser. He gave subjects a candle, a box of thumbtacks, and a book of matches and asked them to find a way to affix the candle to the wall so that when it was lit, wax would not drip onto the floor. Many people had a hard time realizing that the answer was to empty the box of tacks, attach the candle to the inside of the box with melted wax, and then tack the box to the wall. The box acts as a shelf that supports the candle and catches the dripping wax. Because the box had been presented to subjects as a tack holder, they couldn't see it any other way.

In similar puzzles—known by cognitive psychologists as *insight problems*—people have trouble seeing that in a pinch, a plastic lawn chair could be used as a paddle (turn it over, grab two legs, and start rowing); that a basketball could be deflated, formed into the shape of a bowl, and used to safely carry hot coals from one campsite to another; or that a candlewick could be used to tie things together (scrape the wax away to free the string).

What causes functional fixedness? When we see a common object, we automatically screen out awareness of features that are unimportant for its use. This screening is an efficient neurological tactic for everyday life, but it's the enemy of innovation.

One way to overcome the problem is to change how you describe an object. When told that a candlewick is a string, for instance, almost everyone recognizes that it could be used to tie things together. Our *generic parts technique* is a systematic way to change how an object is described. By avoiding unintentionally narrowing people's conception of the object, we open them up to more ideas for its uses.

We consider each element of an object in turn and ask two questions: Can it be broken down further? And does our description imply a particular use? If the answer to either question is yes, we keep breaking down the elements until they're described in their most general terms, mapping the results on a simple tree. When an iceberg is described generically as a floating surface 200 to 400 feet long, its potential as a lifesaving platform soon emerges.

Calling something a wick implies its use as a conduit of a flame. Describing it as a string strips away a layer of preconceived uses and suggests less common ones. Breaking the string down further into its constituent parts of fibrous strands might spark even more uses.

To see if the use of generic descriptions bolsters creative thinking, our research team presented two groups of students with eight insight problems that required overcoming the functional fixedness bias for their solution. We told the members of one group simply to try their best. We taught the other group the generic-parts technique and then asked them to use it on the problems. The people in the first group solved, on average, 49% of the problems (just shy of four of them). Those who systematically created generic descriptions of their resources solved, on average, 83% (or 6.64) of them.

Design Fixation

Simple insight problems given in a psychology lab can be solved by focusing on only four types of features— materials, size, shape, and parts. But solutions to real-world engineering problems often depend on noticing unusual aspects of a broader range of features. This wide-open, imaginative outlook, as we noted, is difficult to develop.

We studied this phenomenon by asking 15 people to list as many features and associations as they could for a candle, a broom, and a dozen other common objects. We then classified their responses by the type of feature, including its color, shape, material, designed use, aesthetic properties, along with the emotions it evokes, the type of energy it generates, and the other objects that the original object is commonly paired with. On average, participants overlooked almost 21 of the 32 types of features (about 65%) that we had previously identified for each object.

Why? When handed a product and asked to create a new design or variation on it, people tend to fixate on the features of the current design. This obstacle to novelty is called *design fixation*. To take a real-world example, when people are shown a sturdy, resealable pouch full of candy and asked to think of a new design that could lead to new uses, they tend to manipulate the types of features used to create the current design. That is, they focus on the width of the base of the pouch or the rigidity of the plastic that makes it stand. To be truly innovative, however, you need to manipulate the features that everyone else has overlooked (see figure 12-1).

But how do you do that? Just as airline pilots have long used checklists to make sure they don't skip any necessary steps when preparing for flight, we developed a checklist of types of product features that people tend to overlook. Whether your product is a physical object or an intangible process, we recommend that you develop a checklist of features that were important to your previous and current innovation projects and add to the list with each new project. Teams working on innovation projects can then refer to the list to prompt them to consider features they would probably otherwise overlook—thus saving time, effort, and frustration.

Examining the pouch of candy with our checklist in mind permitted us to easily uncover many features that could lead to new designs and new uses. First, every pouch sold contains something. This feature is so obvious that its absence is commonly overlooked. Why not sell empty pouches so that customers can decide what to use them for: jewelry, spare change, nuts and bolts, cosmetics, and so on? Imagine empty pouches next to the sandwich bags, freezer bags, and storage bags in your supermarket. Second, most pouches sold are about the size of your hand. Systematically considering changes to the size triggers new ideas for possible contents. What about selling a gallon of paint in a resealable pouch, for instance? Third, current pouches have one inner compartment. But what might you do with more? You could,

FIGURE 12-1

Promising features for a plastic resealable candy package

If you consider an object's less obvious characteristics, new purposes may arise. Here are some features to consider for a candy pouch.

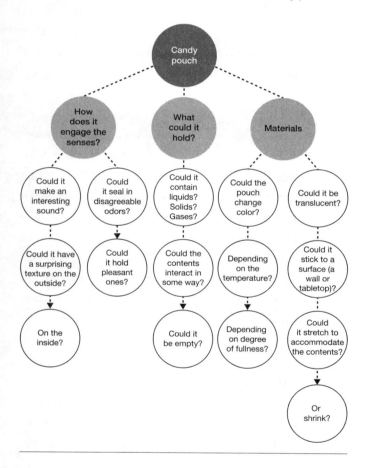

say, sell two-compartment pouches for things you want to mix together later: cereal in the top compartment and milk in the bottom, salad in the bottom and dressing in the top, and so on. Fourth, consider the pouch as a container of a scent (either a good or a bad smell). You could sell a large pouch as a garbage can that reseals to keep in the odor. These are just a few of the new designs that emerge from contemplating a checklist of overlooked features.

Goal Fixedness

Suppose we asked you to think of a way to adhere something to a garbage can. Chances are that like most people, you would think of using glue or tape, both forms of adhesives. But what if we asked you instead to *fasten* something to the can? Just switching a specific verb like *adhere* to a more general one would most likely prompt you to list a wider range of possibilities: binder clip, paper clip, nail, string, Velcro, and so on. That's because the way a goal is phrased often narrows people's thinking. We call this barrier *goal fixedness*. Framing a problem in more general terms can help you overcome this form of fixedness.

But what constitutes a more general term? Is *fasten* more general than *adhere*? A good resource for mapping terms is a thesaurus that makes hierarchical structure explicit by identifying *hyponyms*—more-specific synonyms—for a term. For example, the online thesaurus WordNet indicates that there are least 61 ways to fasten things—including sew, clamp, chain, garter, strap, hook, staple, belt, screw, wire, buckle, cement, tack,

FIGURE 12-2

What's in a name?

How broadly—or narrowly—you phrase a goal affects how you visualize it.

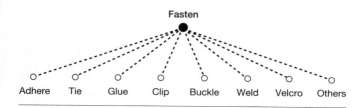

joggle, button, and rivet (figure 12-2). Each method describes the concept of fastening one thing to another in a slightly different way and gives rise to diverse solutions. *Adhere*, by contrast, has only four hyponyms.

Action words, the centerpiece of most goals, often have hyponyms. Each hyponym hints at a more specific way to achieve the goal. There are 172 hyponyms for the verb *remove*, 50 for *guide*, 46 for *transport*, 115 for *separate*, and—perhaps surprisingly—only 24 for the seemingly very general term *mix*.

Of course, a goal consists of more than just a verb. The verb expresses what sort of change you're after, but nouns express what needs changing, and prepositional phrases express important constraints and relationships between things. Put them all together, and almost any goal can be expressed as a verb (*fasten*), a noun (*something*), and a prepositional phrase (*to a garbage can*). Try it: Increase sales in Massachusetts, reduce vibrations in skis, and so on. By putting your goal in this format and playing with the hyponyms of each of its parts, you can explore diverse approaches to your problem in a simple and cost-effective way.

Here's how the approach worked when one of us (Jim) applied it to the real-world goal of reducing concussions in American football. First he dropped the prepositional phrase *in football* from consideration and focused on the verb and noun: *reduce concussions*. To break free of hidden assumptions, he used WordNet to rephrase the goal in as many ways as possible: *lessen trauma, weaken crash, soften jolt, reduce energy, absorb energy, minimize force, exchange forces, substitute energy, oppose energy, repel energy, lessen momentum*, and so on. Using Google, he performed searches such as "concussions lessen trauma" to see which ways of phrasing the goal had been heavily explored already and which ones were underexplored.

Jim found that in the context of concussions, the phrase *repel energy* had relatively few search results—a sign that the solution it implied might have been overlooked. One way to repel energy is through magnets, and this idea suggested a possible approach: Make each helmet magnetic with the same pole so that two helmets would repel each other when near one another. Results from initial tests showed that when the helmets were about to collide they decelerated, and because of their circular shape, they tended to glance off each other, as two magnetic billiard balls would, rather than smashing head-on. Several physicists have verified the plausibility of this approach for significantly reducing the force during helmet collisions.

We began the patenting process for our solution, but our lawyer discovered that someone had submitted the same idea just weeks earlier. We tip our hat to that person.

Visualizing Innovative Thinking

At its most basic level, problem-solving consists of two connected activities: framing a goal and combining resources to accomplish it. Each variation of the goal and every discovery of a "hidden" feature of an available resource can suggest a different course to take. Our approach involves mapping the relationships between all the possibilities in a simple graph, somewhat analogous to a decision tree.

Starting with the goal at the top, we represent each refinement of the goal as a vector pointing downward. The available resources are placed at the bottom, with their features extending upward. Interactions between the resources and their features extend further toward the top. When the two sets of vectors connect, we have a *solution path*. Such a path can be built by working from the top down, by going from the bottom up, or by switching back and forth between the goal and the resources.

This approach is an effective alternative to traditional brainstorming sessions for group innovation work, because it allows people to play to their strengths: Strategically oriented people can focus on refining the goal, while those more familiar with technologies and production processes can begin with the resources. We call this approach *brain-swarming*—a nod to the concept of swarm intelligence. As people contribute to the growing graph, their activity resembles a swarm of insects.

To understand how this visualization approach works, let's return to the problem facing the passengers on the *Titanic*. We'll start with the goal "save passengers." The most obvious resources are the lifeboats. The simplest application of the resources to achieve the goal is "put people in the lifeboats." Thus, we begin with a straight line (see figure 12-3).

FIGURE 12-3

Dominant survival strategy on the *Titanic*

The first step in discovering how resources could be used to reach a goal is to map the most obvious solution.

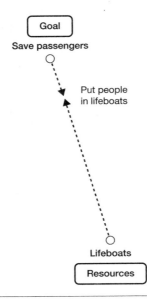

Next, we find different ways to phrase the goal to bring out different solutions. For instance, slightly different goals would be to keep people warm and breathing and to keep people out of the water. Let's look closer at one of these options: keep people out of the water. One way to keep them out of the water is to place them on floating things—not just lifeboats. This idea might spark a fuller consideration of the resources at hand. You might realize that since wood can float, for instance, wooden tables might have been of help. Planks, or perhaps doors, from the ship might have been placed between the lifeboats to hold more people out of the water.

Moving from floating things to even more general considerations of buoyancy might bring to mind the many steamer trunks on board. Tying a set of trunks together to produce another sort of makeshift floating platform might have been enough to support several people directly or to provide a foundation on which to build a more secure platform of wooden planks.

It was estimated that as many as 40 cars were on board. That means 160 tires and inner tubes (not to mention spare tires) were at the passengers' disposal. Tying together rubber tires and inner tubes might conceivably have created a floating raft on which wooden boards could have been placed. And of course, the iceberg itself is a giant floating thing.

On that April night in 1912, none of these ideas might have worked, particularly since it took so long for people to understand the peril they were in. But the point of such an exercise is not to discover the right solution; it is to uncover as many connections between the goal and the widest possible view of the features of the available resources so that you can look beyond the obvious (see figure 12-4).

The goal of the brain-swarming graph, therefore, is to distill the problem-solving process to its most basic components and show how they are all related to one another. People do not have to remember all the com-

FIGURE 12-4

Overlooked strategies for saving *Titanic* passengers

Find new ways to name the goal, and new resources may present themselves.

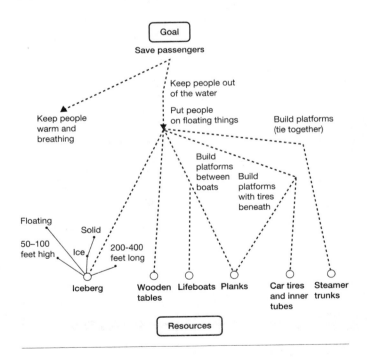

ponents under consideration, because the graph shows them in a glance. This systematic approach takes some of the mystery out of innovation.

In our research, we are discovering that barriers to innovation are like gravity—pervasive, predictable, and not all that strong. There are many ways to overcome them, but the simplest and easiest path is to help your innovators notice what they're overlooking. Often it's right in front of their eyes.

———————

Tony McCaffrey was formerly the chief technology officer of Innovation Accelerator. **Jim Pearson** was formerly the CEO of Innovation Accelerator.

CHAPTER 13

Need Fresh Ideas? Call a Virtual Meeting

by Bob Frisch and Cary Greene

Andrew, the CEO of a $500 million manufacturer, needed to pivot. His company's largest and most reliable revenue source had suddenly dried up. He thought that major changes in focus were required. His team would need to move quickly to sell a different mix of products to different customers.

Andrew set up a videoconference with his 12 direct reports and asked for their help in identifying pools of

Adapted from "3 Things Virtual Meetings Offer That In-Person Meetings Don't" on hbr.org, July 23, 2020 (product #H05Q40).

opportunity. With the press of a button, the executives found themselves in one of three virtual breakout rooms. Each group was tasked with highlighting five pressing market needs the company might be in a position to meet. Andrew had assigned people carefully and appointed leaders for each room; for example, he put the three most opinionated, extroverted leaders with the most forceful facilitator and left more-reserved reports with one another. Each team had a virtual whiteboard for capturing ideas. Andrew moved from one virtual room to another, spending a few minutes listening and commenting before providing some brief coaching points and moving on. After 30 minutes, the attendees were transported back to the main session.

As the spokesperson from each breakout read out the group's top five potential opportunities, a master list of customer needs was captured live and appeared on everyone's screen. A brief question-and-answer session ensured that the ideas were understood. Similar ones were consolidated. Some were refined.

Within an hour of starting the meeting, Andrew was staring at a good list: nine potentially promising areas for growth, four of which had never occurred to him. He shared his screen, displaying a three-by-three matrix of boxes, and asked team members to use the annotation function to initial the box in which they thought each new idea should fall. For the first idea, everyone landed in one of two boxes, as illustrated in figure 13-1.

Andrew called on a few people to explain their placements, and after a quick conversation, the group agreed that the idea was "medium-high"—something they could

FIGURE 13-1

A team vote on where a new idea should fall along two criteria

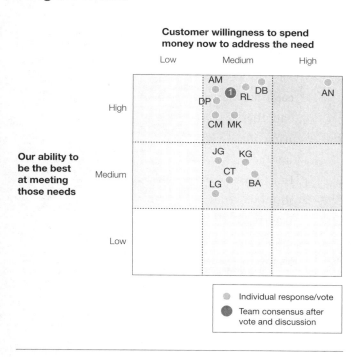

do well but for which customer willingness to pay seemed mixed.

Andrew then read the second idea and asked, "Relative to the first one, where should this idea be placed?" Team members again cast their votes. They repeated the exercise seven times, spending five to 10 minutes on each idea. If team members differed in their views, Andrew asked them to argue their preferences before determining a consensus placement. The result is shown in figure 13-2.

FIGURE 13-2

A team vote on where nine total new ideas should fall along two criteria

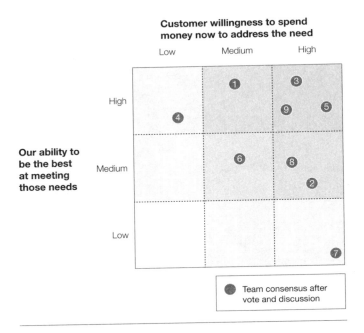

After a 30-minute breakout, a 30-minute reporting period to refine and consolidate ideas, and 75 minutes of discussion, Andrew and his team had pinpointed the three best opportunities to pursue.

Could Andrew have held the same brainstorming session in person? Of course. But doing so would have been far less efficient. Just getting team members to and from breakout areas can take 10 to 15 minutes, and discussions can easily meander over an entire day without a clear conclusion. Three virtual meeting tools—

the whiteboard, the breakout rooms, and the annotation function—combined to give Andrew more control, speed, structure, and clarity than he might have had sitting with his group around a conference table.

Bob Frisch is the founding partner of the Strategic Offsites Group. A regular contributor to *Harvard Business Review*, Bob wrote the bestselling *Who's in the Room? How Great Leaders Structure and Manage the Teams Around Them* and coauthored *Simple Sabotage*. He has earned over 10 million frequent-flier miles facilitating strategy meetings in 19 countries. **Cary Greene** is the managing partner of the Strategic Offsites Group. He is the coauthor of *Simple Sabotage* and a frequent contributor to *Harvard Business Review*, with articles featured across five collections, including *HBR Guide to Making Better Decisions*, *HBR Guide to Making Every Meeting Matter*, and *HBR Guide to Remote Work*.

Creative Collaboration

CHAPTER 14

Set the Conditions for Team Creativity

by Greg Satell

One of the most damaging myths about creativity is that there is a specific creative personality that some people have and others don't. Yet in decades of creativity research, no such trait has ever been identified. The truth is that anybody can be creative, given the right opportunities and context.

If you don't believe me, take the least creative person in your office out for lunch—someone who doesn't seem to have a creative bone in their body. Chances are, you'll find some secret passion, pursued outside of office hours,

Adapted from "Set the Conditions for Anyone on Your Team to Be Creative" on hbr.org, December 5, 2018 (product #H04OSO).

into which they pour their creative energies. They just aren't applying those energies to their day jobs.

The secret to unlocking creativity is not to look for people who are more creative, but to unlock more creativity from the people who already work for you. The same body of creativity research that finds no distinct creative personality is incredibly consistent about what leads to creative work, and they are all things you can implement in your team.

Cultivating Expertise

Over the decades, creativity researchers have consistently found that expertise is absolutely essential for top-notch creative work—and the expertise needs to be specific to a particular field or domain. So the first step to being creative is to become an expert in a particular area.

To understand what a field's important problems are and what would constitute effective new solutions, you need to be an expert. Albert Einstein, for instance, studied physics intensely for years to understand the basic physical model for time and space before he understood that there was an inherent flaw in that model.

So how do you cultivate expertise? Performance expert Anders Ericsson studied that problem for decades and found that the crucial element is deliberate practice. You need to identify the components of a skill, offer coaching, and encourage employees to work on weak areas. This longer-term, continuous approach goes far beyond the intermittent training that most organizations do.

For example, one skill that Amazon has identified as crucial to performance is writing. Employees need to constantly write six-page memos, even for introducing small product features, throughout their careers at the company. They consistently receive coaching and feedback and need to write good memos to advance within the company.

Any company can replicate Amazon's memo-writing policy. What's not so easily replicated is the company's intense, long-term commitment to cultivating writing expertise.

Encouraging Exploration

While deep expertise in a given field is essential for real creativity, it is not sufficient. Look at any great body of creative work, and you'll find a crucial insight that came from outside the original domain. It is often a seemingly random piece of insight that transforms ordinary work into something very different. For example, a random visit to a museum inspired Pablo Picasso's African period. Charles Darwin spent years studying fossils and thinking about evolution until he came across a 40-year-old economics essay by Thomas Malthus. The essay led to Darwin's theory of natural selection. And the philosophy of David Hume helped lead Einstein to special relativity.

More recently, a team of researchers analyzing 17.9 million scientific papers found that the most highly cited work is far more likely to come from a team of experts in one field working with a specialist in something very different. That combination of expertise, exploration, and collaboration is what leads to truly breakthrough ideas.

Empowering Your People with Technology

In Walter Isaacson's biography of Leonardo da Vinci, he recounts how the medieval master would study nature, including anatomy and geological formations, to guide his art. Now, Leonardo was clearly a genius of historical proportions, but think about how much more efficient he would have been with a decent search engine.

One of the most overlooked aspects of innovation is the degree to which technology can enhance productivity. For one thing, technology greatly helps people acquire domain expertise and explore adjacencies. For another, it frees up time to allow for more experimentation.

You can see the power of technology at work at Pixar, which was originally a technology company that began shooting short films to demonstrate the capabilities of its original product, animation software. However, as the company was experimenting with the technology, it also found itself experimenting with storytelling, and those experiments led Pixar to become one of the most highly acclaimed studios in history.

As Pixar cofounder Ed Catmull put it in his memoir, *Creativity, Inc.*, "Every one of our films, when we start off, they suck. . . . Our job is to take it from something that sucks to something that doesn't suck. That's the hard part." This is the kind of continual iteration that technology facilitates—and that makes truly great creative work possible.

Rewarding Persistence

Far too often, we think of creativity as an initial brilliant spark followed by a straightforward period of execution, but as Catmull's preceding comment shows, that's not true in the least. In his book, he calls early ideas "ugly babies" and stresses the need to protect them from being judged too quickly. Yet most organizations do just the opposite. Any idea that doesn't show immediate promise is typically killed quickly and without remorse.

One firm that has been able to buck this trend is IBM. Its research division routinely pursues seemingly outlandish ideas long before they are commercially viable. For example, a team at IBM successfully performed the first quantum teleportation in 1993, when the company was in dire financial straits, with absolutely no financial benefit.

However, the research wasn't particularly expensive, and the company has continued to support the work for decades. Today, it is a leader in quantum computing—a market potentially worth billions—because it stuck with this technology. That's why IBM, despite its ups and downs, remains a highly profitable company while so many of its former rivals are long gone. (See chapter 20 in this book for more on creative persistence.)

Kevin Ashton, who first came up with the idea for RFID chips, encourages persistence in his book *How to Fly a Horse*: "Creation is a long journey, where most turns are wrong and most ends are dead. The most important thing creators do is work. The most important thing they don't do is quit."

Yet all too often, organizations do quit. They expect their babies to be beautiful from the start. They see creation as an event rather than a process, fail to invest in expertise or exploration, and refuse to tolerate wrong turns and dead ends. Is it any wonder that so few companies produce anything truly new and different?

———————

Greg Satell is an international keynote speaker, an adviser, and the bestselling author of *Cascades: How to Create a Movement That Drives Transformational Change* and *Mapping Innovation*. You can learn more about Greg on his website, GregSatell.com, and follow him on Twitter @DigitalTonto.

CHAPTER 15

Why Diverse Teams Are Smarter

by David Rock and Heidi Grant

In recent years, a body of research has revealed a nu-
anced benefit of workplace diversity: Nonhomogeneous
teams are simply smarter. Working with people who are
different from you may challenge your brain to overcome its stale ways of thinking and sharpen its performance and creativity. Let's dig into why diverse teams
are smarter.

They Focus More on Facts

People from diverse backgrounds might actually alter
the behavior of a group's social majority in ways that

Adapted from content posted on hbr.org, November 4, 2016 (product
#H038YZ).

lead to improved and more accurate group thinking. In a study published in the *Journal of Personality and Social Psychology*, scientists assigned 200 people to six-person mock jury panels whose members were either all white or four white and two Black participants. The people were shown a video of a trial of a Black defendant and white victims. They then had to decide whether the defendant was guilty.

It turned out that, compared with the homogeneous panels, the diverse ones raised more facts related to the case and made fewer factual errors when discussing the available evidence. If errors did occur, they were more likely to be corrected during deliberation. One possible reason for this difference was that the white jurors on the diverse panels recalled evidence more accurately.

Other studies have yielded similar results. In a series of experiments conducted by Sheen S. Levine and colleagues in Texas and Singapore, scientists put financially literate people in simulated markets and asked them to price stocks. The participants were placed in either ethnically diverse or homogeneous teams. The researchers found that individuals who were part of the diverse teams were 58% more likely to price stocks correctly, whereas those in homogeneous groups were more prone to pricing errors.

Diverse teams are more likely to constantly reexamine facts and remain objective. They may also encourage greater scrutiny of each member's actions, keeping their joint cognitive resources sharp and vigilant. By breaking up workplace homogeneity, you can allow your employees to become more aware of their own potential biases—entrenched ways of thinking that can otherwise make them miss key information and even lead them to make errors in decision-making processes.

They Process Those Facts More Carefully

Greater diversity may also change the way that entire teams digest information needed to make the best decisions. In a study published in the *Personality and Social Psychology Bulletin*, Katherine Phillips of Northwestern University and her team divided groups of sorority or fraternity members into four-member groups, each of which had to read interviews conducted by a detective investigating a murder. Three people in every group, referred to as "old-timers" in the study, came from the same sorority or fraternity, whereas the fourth, the "newcomer," was either a member of the same sorority or fraternity or a different one. The three old-timers in each group gathered to decide who was the most likely murder suspect. Five minutes into their discussion, the newcomer joined the deliberation and expressed an opinion as to who the suspect was.

Although groups with out-group newcomers felt less confident about the accuracy of their joint decisions, they were more likely to guess who the correct suspect was than were those with newcomers who belonged to the same group.

The scientists think that diverse teams may outperform homogeneous ones in decision-making because these teams process information more carefully. Remember: Considering the perspective of an outsider may seem counterintuitive, but the payoff can be huge.

They're Also More Innovative

To stay competitive, businesses should always continue to innovate. One of the best ways to boost their capacity to transform themselves and their products may involve hiring more women and culturally diverse teams, research suggests. In a study published in *Innovation: Management, Policy & Practice*, Cristina Díaz-García and colleagues analyzed levels of gender diversity in R&D teams from 4,277 companies in Spain. Using statistical models, they found that companies with more women were more likely to introduce radical new innovations into the market over a two-year period.

In another study, published in *Economic Geography*, Max Nathan and Neil Lee concluded that increased cultural diversity is a boon to innovativeness. They pooled data on 7,615 firms that participated in the London Annual Business Survey. This questionnaire asks London executives a number of questions about their companies' performance. The results revealed that businesses run by culturally diverse leadership teams were more likely to develop new products than were those with homogeneous leadership.

Though you may feel more at ease working with people who share your background, don't be fooled by your comfort. Hiring individuals who do not look, talk, or think like you can allow you to dodge the costly pitfalls of conformity, which discourages innovative thinking.

In a nutshell, enriching your employee pool with representatives of different genders, races, and nationalities is key for boosting your company's joint intellectual potential. Creating a more diverse workplace will help to keep your team members' biases in check and make them question their assumptions. At the same time, we need to make sure the organization has inclusive practices so that everyone feels they can be heard. All these efforts to encourage diversity can make your teams smarter and, ultimately, make your organization more successful, whatever your goals.

David Rock is cofounder of the NeuroLeadership Institute and author of *Your Brain at Work*. **Heidi Grant** is a social psychologist who researches, writes, and speaks about the science of motivation. Her most recent book is *Reinforcements: How to Get People to Help You*. She's also the author of *No One Understands You and What to Do About It* and *Nine Things Successful People Do Differently* (Harvard Business Review Press, 2018, 2015, 2012, respectively).

CHAPTER 16

The Most Creative Teams Have a Specific Kind of Cultural Diversity

by Sujin Jang

Culturally diverse teams, research shows, can help deliver better outcomes in today's organizations. This is largely a good thing: Diverse teams have the potential to be more creative because of the breadth of information, ideas, and perspectives that members can bring to the table (see chapter 15). But because these teams often suffer from conflicting norms and differing assumptions

---

Adapted from content posted on hbr.org, July 24, 2018 (product #H04GET).

between members, they don't always reach their full creative potential. When managers don't know how to spot and address these situations, cultural diversity may actually inhibit a team's creative performance.

The Importance of Cultural Brokers

My research, which was published in *Organization Science*, finds that *cultural brokerage* is a key factor that allows multicultural teams to capitalize on the benefits of diversity while mitigating the pitfalls. I define cultural brokerage as the act of facilitating interactions across parties from different cultural backgrounds. In two studies—an archival study of over 2,000 multicultural teams and an experiment involving 83 multicultural teams with different cultural compositions—I found that teams were significantly more creative when they had one or more members who acted as a cultural broker.

Who are these cultural brokers? They're team members who have relatively more multicultural experience than others do and who act as a bridge between their monocultural teammates. These brokers come in two profiles. First, they can have multicultural experiences that map directly onto the cultures they are bridging. For example, in a team with mostly Indian and American team members, a cultural broker could be someone with experience in both Indian and American cultures. I call such individuals *cultural insiders*. The second type of cultural broker is someone with experience in two or more cultures not represented in the team—say, Australian and Korean. I call such individuals *cultural outsiders*.

I found that cultural insiders and outsiders each draw on their distinct cultural backgrounds relative to the team to engage in different kinds of cultural brokerage. In the experimental study, cultural insiders used their dual knowledge of the other cultures on their team to integrate information and ideas from those cultures. In other words, they often proposed ideas that combined elements of both cultures. Meanwhile, cultural outsiders drew on their position as a neutral third party to elicit information and ideas from the other cultures represented in the team. They tended to ask questions of other team members and invite them to share relevant cultural knowledge. Both types of cultural brokerage led to a boost in creativity at the team level.

Why Cultural Diversity Alone Is Not Enough

First and foremost, this research suggests that it is not enough to simply bring together people from different cultures and expect them to produce creative outcomes. For teams to unleash their full creative potential, they need at least one multicultural insider or outsider in the group. Outsider cultural brokers, I suspect, may be less common in organizations, because many people incorrectly assume only those with culture-specific knowledge are in a position to facilitate cross-cultural interactions. In fact, however, cultural outsiders are just as effective as cultural insiders are in enhancing team creativity. This is particularly good news for highly diverse teams, which are unlikely to have a single cultural insider.

At the same time, you cannot simply assign someone to be a cultural broker and call it day. A formal appointment does not guarantee that a person will be effective; instead, organizations should take care to create the conditions that can allow cultural brokerage to emerge. Remember, being a broker requires substantial cognitive and emotional effort. Because of these requirements, effective cultural brokerage is more likely to emerge in teams with a high level of psychological safety. It also requires active participation and buy-in from the team as a whole and is more likely to emerge in teams that view diversity as a resource and a source of learning.

Collaboration in multicultural teams is a complex and multifaceted endeavor. While this type of work can be challenging, my research suggests that understanding the dynamics of cultural brokerage provides a critical advantage in realizing the creative potential of diverse teams.

———————

Sujin Jang is an assistant professor of organisational behaviour at INSEAD. Her research focuses on global teams and the challenges of working across cultures.

CHAPTER 17

How to Cultivate Psychological Safety on Your Team

by Laura Delizonna

"There's no team without trust," says Paul Santagata, head of industry at Google. He knows the results of the tech giant's massive two-year study on team performance, which revealed that the highest-performing teams have one thing in common: psychological safety, the belief that you won't be punished when you make a

---

Adapted from "High-Performing Teams Need Psychological Safety: Here's How to Create It" on hbr.org, August 24, 2017 (product #H03TK7).

mistake. Studies show that psychological safety allows for moderate risk-taking, speaking your mind, creativity, and sticking your neck out without fear of having it cut off—just the types of behavior that lead to market breakthroughs.

Ancient evolutionary adaptations explain why psychological safety is both fragile and vital to success in uncertain, interdependent environments. The brain processes a provocation by a boss, a competitive coworker, or a dismissive subordinate as a life-and-death threat. The amygdala, the alarm bell in the brain, ignites the fight-or-flight response, hijacking higher brain centers. This "act first, think later" brain structure shuts down perspective and analytical reasoning. Quite literally, just when we need it most, we lose our minds. While that fight-or-flight reaction may save us in life-and-death situations, it handicaps the strategic thinking needed in today's workplace.

Twenty-first-century success depends on another system—the broaden-and-build mode of positive emotion, which allows us to solve complex problems and foster cooperative relationships. Barbara Fredrickson at the University of North Carolina has found that positive emotions like trust, curiosity, confidence, and inspiration broaden the mind and help us build psychological, social, and physical resources. We become more open-minded, resilient, motivated, and persistent when we feel safe. Humor increases, as does our ability to find solutions and apply divergent thinking—the cognitive process underlying creativity.

When the workplace feels challenging but not threatening, teams can sustain the broaden-and-build mode. Oxytocin levels in our brains rise, eliciting trust and trust-making behavior. Trust is a huge factor in team success, as Santagata attests: "In Google's fast-paced, highly demanding environment, our success hinges on the ability to take risks and be vulnerable in front of peers."

So how can you increase psychological safety on your own team? Try replicating the steps that Santagata took with his.

We humans hate losing even more than we love winning. A perceived loss triggers attempts to reestablish fairness through competition, criticism, or disengagement, which is a form of workplace-learned helplessness. Santagata knows that true success is a win-win outcome, so when conflicts come up, he avoids triggering a fight-or-flight reaction by asking, "How could we achieve a mutually desirable outcome?"

Underlying every team's who-did-what confrontation are universal needs such as respect, competence, social status, and autonomy. Recognizing these deeper needs naturally elicits trust and promotes positive language and behaviors. Santagata reminded his team that even in the most contentious negotiations, the other party is just like them and aims to walk away happy. He led them through a reflection called Just Like Me, which asks you to consider these likely observations:

- This person has beliefs, perspectives, and opinions, just like me.

- This person has hopes, anxieties, and vulnerabilities, just like me.

- This person has friends, family, and perhaps children who love them, just like me.

- This person wants to feel respected, appreciated, and competent, just like me.

- This person wishes for peace, joy, and happiness, just like me.

"Thinking through in advance how your audience will react to your messaging helps ensure your content will be heard, versus your audience hearing an attack on their identity or ego," explains Santagata.

Skillfully confront difficult conversations head-on by preparing for likely reactions. For example, you may need to gather concrete evidence to counter defensiveness when discussing hot-button issues. Santagata asks himself, "If I position my point in this manner, what are the possible objections, and how would I respond to those counterarguments?" He says, "Looking at the discussion from this third-party perspective exposes weaknesses in my positions and encourages me to rethink my argument." Specifically, he asks three questions:

- What are my main points?

- What are three ways my listeners are likely to respond?

- How will I respond to each of those scenarios?

If team members sense that you're trying to blame them for something, you become their saber-toothed tiger. John Gottman's research at the University of Washington shows that blame and criticism reliably escalate conflict, leading to defensiveness and—eventually—to disengagement. The alternative to blame is curiosity. If you believe you already know what the other person is thinking, then you're not ready to have a conversation. Instead, adopt a learning mindset, knowing you don't have all the facts. Here's how:

- State the problematic behavior or outcome as an observation, and use factual, neutral language. For example, "In the past two months, there's been a noticeable drop in your participation during meetings, and progress appears to be slowing on your project."

- Engage them in an exploration. For example, "I imagine there are multiple factors at play. Perhaps we could uncover what they are together?"

- Ask for solutions. The people who are responsible for creating a problem often hold the keys to solving it. That's why a positive outcome typically depends on their input and buy-in. Ask directly, "What do you think needs to happen here?" Or, "What would be your ideal scenario?" Another question leading to solutions is, "How could I support you?"

Asking for feedback on how you delivered your message disarms your opponent, illuminates blind spots in communication skills, and models fallibility. All of these results increase trust in leaders. Santagata closes difficult conversations with these questions:

- What worked and what didn't work in my delivery?

- How did it feel to hear this message?

- How could I have presented it more effectively?

For example, Santagata asked about his delivery after giving his senior manager tough feedback. His manager replied, "This could have felt like a punch in the stomach, but you presented reasonable evidence, and that made me want to hear more. You were also eager to discuss the challenges I had, which led to solutions."

Santagata periodically asks his team how safe they feel and what could enhance their feeling of safety. In addition, his team routinely takes surveys on psychological safety and other team dynamics. Some teams at Google include questions such as, "How confident are you that you won't receive retaliation or criticism if you admit an error or make a mistake?"

If you create this sense of psychological safety on your own team starting now, you can expect to see higher levels of engagement. Your group will also enjoy increased motivation for tackling difficult problems, more learning and development opportunities, and better performance.

Laura Delizonna is an executive coach, an instructor at Stanford University, a keynote speaker, and a culture consultant at Delizonna.com. She specializes in equipping leaders of top companies with the frameworks and tools to build high-performance cultures.

CHAPTER 18

How to Give and Receive Feedback About Creative Work

by Spencer Harrison

Feedback is crucial for learning and improving, but we rarely enjoy being on the receiving end of it when it's criticism. Many people have a negative reaction to feedback, especially feedback on their creative work. In a study of seven companies and 11,471 days of creative work, Harvard Business School professor Teresa M. Amabile and her colleagues found two striking patterns:

Adapted from content posted on hbr.org, November 13, 2017 (product #H040EK).

First, getting feedback was incredibly rare, indicating that people seemed to avoid it. And second, when people did receive feedback, it generally left a negative emotional residue.

So, what might good feedback for creative work look like? By *good feedback*, I mean feedback that people actually want and that leads to changes that improve their creative output.

Identifying how to do this requires understanding how creativity works. Creativity is the generation of an idea that is both useful and novel. Combining the two requires some care because novelty, by definition, is something unfamiliar to both the creator and anyone seeing the idea for the first time. As a result, early creative ideas can be fragile and dismissed as too new, weird, or unnecessary. New ideas need direction that can build them up, rather than critiques that can tear them down.

At the same time, creativity does require feedback. As much as we have mythologized creativity as the domain of an individual genius working alone, almost all creative processes used in organizations—design thinking, lean startup methodologies, agile development, and more—benefit from feedback early on. As a result, organizations must provide effective feedback to cultivate creative ideas; it's one of the ways for them to adapt to industry changes and competitive pressures. Leaders will want to understand how to give and receive feedback effectively in creative work.

Karyn Dossinger and I have published research that gets at this question, focusing on a successful online company that crowdsources T-shirt designs from a large community of freelance designers. Its website hosts a forum where designers can ask for feedback on early design prototypes from their peers and then post updated designs based on the comments they received. Looking across almost 2,000 feedback statements, we learned that two dynamics seem crucial: First, designers who were motivated to seek feedback out of curiosity, as opposed to simply improving their design, attracted more and higher-quality feedback. Second, the peer critics who recognized that feedback is a subjective opinion as opposed to an objective statement were more effective in enhancing the creativity of the final design. Let's examine these two dynamics.

Asking for Feedback Out of Curiosity

How we ask for people's opinions influences the scope and type of feedback we receive. Sometimes the requests are overly narrow. For example, we found that some T-shirt designers asked about the color of a dinosaur they had illustrated, their font choice, or the placement of a monkey working on a typewriter. There are often underlying reasons for asking a specific question like this. You might, for example, be trying to restrain a coworker from attacking your work, or perhaps you're showcasing something you're proud of (in which case you really don't want feedback—you want admiration).

This narrow approach, however, limits the potential of creative work, because it doesn't allow for the possibility of novelty. Changing one color, for example, may not push the boundaries to create something that peers and potential customers haven't seen before.

Our research showed that highly curious individuals asked extremely open questions like "What do you think?" or "Where could I go next with this?" These designers received significantly more feedback than those asking narrow questions, and their final designs received higher scores. By leading with curiosity, the feedback seekers signaled an openness to ideas beyond their own and enjoyed the benefits of broader ideas. In contrast, narrow questions signal that the feedback seeker already has a set of ideas and wants validation that those ideas are correct. In this way, creative work is like dancing: Questions born out of curiosity signal that the creative worker is looking for a dance partner. (For more on the business case for curiosity, see chapter 21 of this guide.)

Providing Feedback Based on Subjectivity

If asking questions is like asking for a dance partner, then providing feedback is being the type of dance partner someone would actually want to dance with. A huge part of creativity is this ability to get your audience to agree that what you're doing feels new and surprising to them. And just as asking open questions honors the fact that creativity requires novelty, providing feedback needs to honor that same assumption. It needs to provide space for something new, something that might not be anticipated by either party, to emerge.

When providing feedback to creative workers, signal that your opinion is exactly that: an opinion. This acknowledgment of your subjectivity seems deceptively easy. It requires providing feedback that includes first-person pronouns: *I*, *me*, and *my*. "I see . . ." or "What strikes me is that . . ." or "My opinion is . . ." Many managers find this subjective angle difficult, because they have been trained to solve concrete problems, not to consider what something really means. Providing feedback on creative work means setting aside the managerial impulse to plan and retain control. By speaking from a personal point of view, managers recognize that their opinions provide *potential trajectories* a creative worker might try—not the "right" road to take.

Feedback is tricky, and it's even trickier for creative work. But asking for feedback out of curiosity and basing your feedback on subjectivity can improve both the process and the outcomes.

Spencer Harrison is an associate professor of organisational behaviour at INSEAD. He grew up drawing cartoons, invents stories for his kids, likes using the word *puzzle* as a verb, and researches creativity and how people connect to their work.

CHAPTER 19

Why Design Thinking Works

by Jeanne Liedtka

Occasionally, a new way of organizing work leads to extraordinary improvements. Total quality management did that in manufacturing in the 1980s by combining a set of tools—kanban cards, quality circles, and so on—with the insight that people on the shop floor could do much higher level work than they were usually asked to. That blend of tools and insight, applied to a work process, can be thought of as a *social technology.*

In a seven-year study, I looked in depth at 50 projects from a range of sectors, including business, health care, and social services. I found that another social

---

Adapted from an article in *Harvard Business Review*, September–October 2018 (product #R1805D).

technology, design thinking, has the potential to do for innovation exactly what total quality management did for manufacturing: unleash people's full creative energies, win their commitment, and radically improve processes. By now most executives have at least heard about design thinking's tools—ethnographic research, an emphasis on reframing problems and experimentation, the use of diverse teams, and so on—if not tried them. But what people may not understand is the subtler way that design thinking gets around the human biases (for example, rootedness in the status quo) or attachments to specific behavioral norms ("That's how we do things here") that time and again block the exercise of imagination.

In this chapter, I'll explore a variety of human tendencies that get in the way of innovation, and I'll describe how design thinking's tools and clear process steps help teams break free of them. Let's begin by looking at what organizations need from innovation—and at why their efforts to obtain it often fall short.

The Challenges of Innovation

To be successful, an innovation process must deliver three things: superior solutions, lower risks and costs of change, and employee buy-in. Over the years, businesspeople have developed useful tactics for achieving those outcomes. But when trying to apply them, organizations frequently encounter new obstacles and trade-offs.

Superior solutions

Defining problems in obvious, conventional ways, not surprisingly, often leads to obvious, conventional solutions. *Asking a more interesting question* can help teams discover more-original ideas. The risk is that some teams may get indefinitely hung up exploring a problem, while action-oriented managers may be too impatient to take the time to figure out what question they should be asking.

It's also widely accepted that solutions are much better when they incorporate *user-driven criteria*. Market research can help companies understand those criteria, but the hurdle here is that it's hard for customers to know they want something that doesn't yet exist.

Finally, bringing *diverse voices* into the process is also known to improve solutions. This can be difficult to manage, however, if conversations among people with opposing views deteriorate into divisive debates.

Lower risks and costs

Uncertainty is unavoidable in innovation. That's why innovators often build a *portfolio of options*. The trade-off is that a portfolio of too many ideas dilutes focus and resources. To manage this tension, innovators must be willing to let go of bad ideas—to "call the baby ugly," as a manager in one of my studies described it. Unfortunately, people often find it easier to kill the creative (and arguably riskier) ideas than to kill the incremental ones.

Employee buy-in

An innovation won't succeed unless a company's employees get behind it. The surest route to winning their support is to involve them in the generation of ideas. The danger is that the involvement of many people with different perspectives will create chaos and incoherence.

Underlying the trade-offs associated with achieving these outcomes is a more fundamental tension. In a stable environment, organizations achieve efficiency by driving variation out of their processes. But in an unstable world, variation becomes the organization's friend because it opens new paths to success. However, who can blame leaders who must meet quarterly targets for doubling down on efficiency, rationality, and centralized control?

To manage all the trade-offs, organizations need a social technology that addresses these behavioral obstacles and the counterproductive biases of human beings. And as I'll explain next, design thinking fits that bill.

The Beauty of Structure

Experienced designers often complain that design thinking is too structured and linear. And for them, that's certainly true. But managers on innovation teams are generally not designers. They're not used to doing face-to-face research with customers, getting deeply immersed in their perspectives, cocreating with stakeholders, and designing and executing experiments. Structure and linearity help managers try to adjust to these new behaviors.

As Kaaren Hanson, formerly the head of design innovation at Intuit and now chief design officer at JPMorgan Chase, explains, "Anytime you're trying to change people's behavior, you need to start them off with a lot of structure, so they don't have to think. A lot of what we do is habit, and it's hard to change those habits, but having very clear guardrails can help us."

Organized processes keep people on track and curb the tendency to spend too long exploring a problem or to impatiently skip ahead. They also instill confidence. Most humans are driven by a fear of mistakes, so they focus more on preventing errors than on seizing opportunities. When a choice risks failure, they opt for inaction rather than action. But because there is no innovation without action, psychological safety is essential. The physical props and highly formatted tools of design thinking deliver that sense of security, helping would-be innovators move more assuredly through the discovery of customer needs, idea generation, and idea testing.

In most organizations the application of design thinking involves seven activities. Each generates a clear output that the next activity converts to another output until the organization arrives at an implementable innovation. But at a deeper level, something else is happening—something that executives are generally unaware of. Though ostensibly geared to understanding and molding the experiences of customers, each design-thinking activity also profoundly reshapes the experiences of the *innovators themselves*.

Customer Discovery

Many of the best-known methods of the design-thinking discovery process relate to identifying the "job to be done." Adapted from the fields of ethnography and sociology, these methods concentrate on examining what makes for a meaningful customer journey rather than focusing on the collection and analysis of data. This exploration entails three sets of activities.

Immersion

Traditionally, customer research has been an impersonal exercise. An expert, who may well have preexisting theories about customer preferences, reviews feedback from focus groups, surveys, and, if available, data on current behavior and draws inferences about customer needs. The better the data, the better the inferences. The trouble is, this approach grounds people in the already-articulated needs that the data reflects. They see the data through the lens of their own biases. And they don't recognize needs that people have *not* expressed.

Design thinking takes a different approach: The innovator identifies hidden needs by living the customer's experience. Consider what happened at the Kingwood Trust, a U.K. charity helping adults with autism and Asperger's syndrome. One design team member, Katie Gaudion, got to know Pete, a nonverbal adult with autism. The first time she observed him at his home, she saw him engaged in seemingly damaging acts—like picking at a leather sofa and rubbing indents in a wall. She started by documenting Pete's behavior and defined the problem as how to prevent such destructiveness.

But on her second visit to Pete's home, she asked herself, "What if Pete's actions were motivated by something other than a destructive impulse?" Putting her personal perspective aside, she mirrored his behavior and discovered how satisfying his activities actually felt. "Instead of a ruined sofa, I now perceived Pete's sofa as an object wrapped in fabric that is fun to pick," she explained. "Pressing my ear against the wall and feeling the vibrations of the music above, I felt a slight tickle in my ear whilst rubbing the smooth and beautiful indentation. . . . So instead of a damaged wall, I perceived it as a pleasant and relaxing audio-tactile experience."

Gaudion's immersion in Pete's world not only produced a deeper understanding of his challenges but also called into question an unexamined bias about the residents, who had been perceived as disability sufferers who needed to be kept safe. Her experience caused her to ask herself another new question: Instead of designing just for residents' disabilities and safety, how could the innovation team design for their strengths and pleasures? That led to the creation of living spaces, gardens, and new activities aimed at enabling people with autism to live fuller and more pleasurable lives. Table 19-1 summarizes how innovators take on this immersive approach.

Sense making

Immersion in user experiences provides raw material for deeper insights. But finding patterns and making sense of the mass of qualitative data collected is a daunting challenge. Time and again, I have seen initial enthusiasm about the results of ethnographic tools fade as nondesigners become overwhelmed by the volume of information and the messiness of searching for deeper insights. It is here that the structure of design thinking really comes into its own.

TABLE 19-1

Shaping the innovator's journey

What makes design thinking a social technology is its ability to counteract the biases of innovators and change the way they engage in the innovation process.

Problem	Design thinking	Improved outcome
Innovators are trapped in their own expertise and experience.	Design thinking provides immersion in the user's experience, shifting an innovator's mindset toward . . .	. . . a better understanding of those being designed for.
Innovators feel overwhelmed by the volume and messiness of qualitative data.	Design thinking makes sense of data by organizing it into themes and patterns, pointing the innovator toward . . .	. . . new insights and possibilities.
Innovators are divided by differences in team members' perspectives.	Design thinking builds alignment as insights are translated into design criteria, moving an innovation team toward . . .	. . . convergence around what really matters to users.
Innovators are confronted by too many disparate but familiar ideas.	Design thinking encourages the emergence of fresh ideas through a focused inquiry, shifting team members toward . . .	. . . a limited but diverse set of potential new solutions.
Innovators are constrained by existing biases about what does or doesn't work.	Design thinking fosters articulation of the conditions necessary to each idea's success and transitions a team toward . . .	. . . clarity on make-or-break assumptions; enables the design of meaningful experiments.
Innovators lack a shared understanding of new ideas and are often unable to get good feedback from users.	Design thinking offers pre-experiences to users through rough prototypes that help innovators get . . .	. . . accurate feedback at low cost and an understanding of potential solutions' true value.
Innovators fear change and ambiguity surrounding the new future.	Design thinking delivers learning in action as experiments engage staff and users, helping them build . . .	. . . a shared commitment and confidence in the new product or strategy.

One of the most effective ways to make sense of the knowledge generated by immersion is a design-thinking exercise called the gallery walk. In this exercise, the core innovation team selects the most important data gathered during the discovery process and writes it down on large posters. Often these posters showcase individuals who have been interviewed, complete with their photos and quotations capturing their perspectives. The posters are hung around a room, and key stakeholders are invited to tour this gallery and write down on Post-it notes the bits of data they consider essential to new designs. The stakeholders then form small teams, and in a carefully orchestrated process, their Post-it observations are shared, combined, and sorted by theme into clusters that the group mines for insights. This process overcomes the danger that innovators will be unduly influenced by their own biases and see only what they want to see, because it makes the people who were interviewed feel vivid and real to those browsing the gallery. The exercise creates a common database and facilitates collaborators' ability to interact, reach shared insights together, and challenge one another's individual takeaways—another critical guard against biased interpretations.

Alignment

The final stage in the discovery process is a series of workshops and seminar discussions that ask some form of this question: If anything were possible, what job would the design do well? The focus on possibilities rather than on the constraints imposed by the status quo helps diverse teams have more-collaborative and creative discussions about the design criteria, that is, the key features that an ideal innovation should have. Establishing a spirit of inquiry deepens dissatisfaction with the status quo and makes it easier for teams to reach consensus throughout the innovation process. And down the road, when the portfolio of ideas is winnowed, agreement on the design criteria will give novel ideas a fighting chance against safer, incremental ones.

Consider what happened at Monash Health, an integrated hospital and health-care system in Melbourne, Australia. Mental health clinicians there had long been concerned about the frequency of patient relapses—usually in the form of drug overdoses and suicide attempts—but consensus on how to address this problem eluded them. In an effort to get to the bottom of it, clinicians traced the experiences of specific patients through their treatment. One patient, Tom, emerged as emblematic in their study. His experience included three face-to-face visits with different clinicians, 70 touchpoints, 13 different case managers, and 18 handoffs during the interval between his initial visit and his relapse.

The team members held a series of workshops in which they asked clinicians this question: Did Tom's current care exemplify why they had entered health care? As people discussed their motivations for becoming doctors and nurses, they came to realize that improving Tom's outcome might depend as much on their sense of duty to Tom himself as it did on their clinical activity. Everyone bought into this conclusion, which made designing a new treatment process—centered on the patient's needs rather than perceived best practices—proceed smoothly and successfully. After its implementation, patient-relapse rates fell by 60%.

Idea Generation

Once they understand customers' needs, innovators move on to identify and winnow down specific solutions that conform to the criteria they've identified.

Emergence

The first step here is to set up a dialogue about potential solutions, carefully planning who will participate, what challenge they will be given, and how the conversation will be structured. After using the design criteria to do some individual brainstorming, participants gather to share ideas and build on them creatively—as opposed to simply negotiating compromises when differences arise.

When Children's Health System of Texas, the sixth-largest pediatric medical center in the United States, identified the need for a new strategy, the organization, led by the vice president of population health, Peter Roberts, applied design thinking to reimagine its business model. During the discovery process, clinicians set aside their bias that what mattered most was medical intervention. They came to understand that intervention alone wouldn't work if the local population in Dallas lacked the time or ability to seek out medical knowledge and had no strong support networks—something few families in the area enjoyed. The clinicians also realized that the medical center couldn't successfully address problems on its own; the community would need to be central to any solution. So Children's Health invited its community partners to codesign a new wellness ecosystem whose boundaries (and resources) would stretch far beyond the medical center. Deciding to start small and tackle a single condition, the team gathered to create a new model for managing asthma.

The session brought together hospital administrators, physicians, nurses, social workers, parents of patients, and staff from Dallas's school districts, its housing authority, the YMCA, and faith-based organizations around the city. First, the core innovation team shared learning from the discovery process. Next, each attendee thought independently about the capabilities that their own institution might contribute toward addressing the children's problems, jotting down ideas on sticky notes. The participants were then invited to join a small group at one of five tables, where people would share individual ideas, group them into common themes, and envision what an ideal experience would look like for the young patients and their families.

Champions of change usually emerge from these kinds of conversations, and their presence greatly improves the chances of successful implementation. (All too often, good ideas die on the vine in the absence of people with a personal commitment to making them happen.) At Children's Health, the partners invited into the project galvanized the community to act. In their institutions, they also forged and maintained the relationships required to realize the new vision. Housing authority representatives drove changes in housing codes, charging inspectors with incorporating children's health issues (like the presence of mold) into their assessments.

Local pediatricians adopted a set of standard asthma protocols, and parents of children with asthma took on a significant role as peer counselors providing intensive education to other families through home visits.

Articulation

Typically, emergence activities generate several competing ideas, more or less attractive and more or less feasible. In the next step, articulation, innovators uncover and examine their implicit assumptions. Managers are often bad at articulation, because of many behavioral biases, such as overoptimism, confirmation bias, and fixation on first solutions. When assumptions aren't challenged, discussions around what will or won't work become deadlocked, with everyone advocating from their own unique understanding of how the world works.

In contrast, design thinking frames the discussion as an inquiry into what would have to be true about the world for an idea to be feasible. An example of this approach comes from the Ignite Accelerator program of the U.S. Department of Health and Human Services. At the Whiteriver Indian Hospital in Arizona, a team led by Marliza Rivera, a young quality-control officer, sought to reduce the hospital's emergency room wait times, which were sometimes as long as six hours.

The team's initial concept, borrowed from the Johns Hopkins Hospital in Baltimore, was to install an electronic kiosk for check-in. As team members began to apply design thinking, however, they were asked to surface their assumptions about why the idea would work. It was only then that they realized that their patients, many of whom were older Apache speakers, were unlikely to be comfortable with computer technology. Approaches that worked in urban Baltimore would not work in Whiteriver, so this idea could be safely set aside.

At the end of the idea generation process, innovators will have a portfolio of well-thought-out but possibly quite different ideas. The assumptions underlying them will have been carefully vetted, and the conditions necessary for their success will be achievable. The ideas will also have the support of committed teams, who will be prepared to take on the responsibility of bringing them to market.

The Testing Experience

Companies often regard prototyping as a process of fine-tuning a product or service that has already largely been developed. But in design thinking, prototyping is carried out on far-from-finished products. It's about users' iterative experiences with a work in progress. The project's malleable status means that quite radical changes—including complete redesigns—can occur along the way.

Pre-experience

Neuroscience research indicates that helping people *pre-experience* something novel—that is, imagine it incredibly vividly—results in more-accurate assessments of the novelty's value. That's why design thinking calls for the creation of basic, low-cost artifacts that will capture the essential features of the proposed user experience. These are not literal prototypes—and they are often much rougher than the minimum viable products that lean startups test with customers. But what these artifacts lose in fidelity they gain in flexibility, because they can easily be altered in response to what the users learned when exposed to them. And their incompleteness invites interaction.

Such artifacts can take many forms. Designers tested the layout of a new medical office building at Kaiser Permanente, for example, by hanging bedsheets from the ceiling to mark future walls. Nurses and physicians were invited to interact with staffers who were playing the role of patients and to suggest how the spaces could be adjusted to better facilitate treatment. At Monash Health, a program called Monash Watch was aimed at using telemedicine to keep vulnerable populations healthy at home and reduce their hospitalization rates. The designers of the program used detailed storyboards to help hospital administrators and government policy makers envision this new approach in practice, without building a digital prototype.

Learning in action

Real-world experiments are an essential way to assess new ideas and identify the changes needed to make them workable. But such tests offer another, less obvious kind of value: They help reduce employees' and customers' quite normal fear of change.

Consider an idea proposed by Donald Campbell, a professor of medicine, and Keith Stockman, then a manager of operations research at Monash Health. As part of Monash Watch, they suggested hiring laypeople to be telecare guides who would act as "professional neighbors," maintaining frequent telephone contact with patients at high risk of multiple hospital admissions. Campbell and Stockman hypothesized that lower-wage laypeople who were carefully selected, trained in health literacy and empathy skills, and backed by a decision support system and professional coaches the lay guides could involve as needed could help keep the at-risk patients healthy at home.

Their proposal was met with skepticism. Many of their colleagues held a strong bias against letting anyone besides a health professional perform such a service for patients with complex issues, but using health professionals in the role would have been unaffordable. Rather than debating this point, however, the innovation team members acknowledged the concerns and engaged their colleagues in the codesign of an experiment testing that assumption. Three hundred patients later, the results were in: Overwhelmingly positive patient feedback and a demonstrated reduction in bed use and emergency room visits, corroborated by independent consultants, quelled the fears of the skeptics.

As we have seen, the structure of design thinking creates a natural flow from research to rollout. Immersion in the customer experience produces data, which is transformed into insights that help teams agree on the design criteria they use to brainstorm solutions. Assumptions about what's critical to the success of those solutions are examined and then tested with rough prototypes that help teams further develop innovations and prepare them for real-world experiments.

Along the way, design-thinking processes counteract human biases that thwart creativity while addressing the challenges typically faced in reaching superior solutions, lowered costs and risks, and employee buy-in. Recognizing organizations as collections of human beings who are motivated by varying perspectives and emotions, design thinking emphasizes engagement, dialogue, and learning. By involving customers and other stakeholders in the definition of the problem and the development of solutions, design thinking garners a broad commitment to change. And by supplying a structure to the innovation process, design thinking helps innovators collaborate and agree on what is essential to the outcome at every phase. It does this not only by overcoming workplace politics but also by shaping the experiences of the innovators, the key stakeholders, and the key implementers at every step. *That* is social technology at work.

———————

Jeanne Liedtka is a professor of business administration at the University of Virginia's Darden School of Business.

CHAPTER 20

Your Best Ideas Are Often Your Last Ideas

by Loran Nordgren and Brian Lucas

To live up to our creative potential, we must first understand how the creative process actually works. Prior research has shown that people's first ideas are rarely their most creative. Coming up with just one breakthrough idea typically requires a lengthy brainstorming process in which you generate a large pool of potential options and iterate on them before finally reaching your most creative idea.

Adapted from content posted on hbr.org, January 26, 2021 (product #H064S5).

Despite this reality, however, most people consistently underestimate the value of persistence in the creative process. In our research, we document a fallacy we call the *creative cliff illusion*: Although creativity in fact tends to either increase or stay the same across an ideation session, people assume that creativity drops off over time.

We explored this misconception—and what managers can do to overcome it—with a series of studies in which we asked people to predict how their creativity would change over an ideation session. We ran these experiments using a variety of creative problem-solving tasks and across several sample U.S. populations, including university students and working adults.

In one of our studies, we enrolled professional and amateur comedians in a caption-writing competition. We surveyed their beliefs about how creativity changes over time and then had them spend as long as they wanted coming up with captions for a cartoon. We found that the comedians who were more certain that their early ideas would be their best ones stopped ideating sooner. These comedians ended up submitting fewer jokes. And importantly, fewer of their submitted jokes were rated as being highly creative. These results suggest that if you think your first ideas will be your best, you're more likely to stop the creative process before your actual best ideas are uncovered.

Why are people so bad at predicting their own creativity? The answer lies with a performance indicator that is often (falsely) conflated with creativity: productivity. When we are generating ideas (or, for that matter,

GIVING UP IS THE ENEMY OF CREATIVITY

1. Ignore your first instinct to stop. When working on a tough creative challenge, you will be likely to face a moment when you feel stuck and can't come up with any more ideas. You'll first want to quit and spend your time doing something else. Temporarily ignore this instinct, especially if you're still in the early stages of the work. Try to generate just a few more ideas, or consider just a few more alternatives. You may find that your next creative idea was closer than you imagined.

2. Remember that creative problems are supposed to feel difficult. Most involve setbacks, failures, and that stuck feeling. These feelings are part of the process. Suppress your instinct to interpret them as a signal that you just aren't creative or that you've run out of good ideas. Reaching your creative potential will often take time, you'll need persistence to see a challenge through to the end.

Adapted from content posted on hbr.org, December 1, 2015 (product #H02IYX).

when we are completing any task that requires mental energy), productivity does tend to decline over time, and people often take the ease of producing ideas as a signal of the quality of those ideas. Because people recognize that their productivity declines with time, they think the creativity of the ideas they produce must decline as well. But of course, this is not the case. In the creative process, the ideas that are most easily accessed tend to be the most obvious ones. Only by digging deeper do we finally uncover more novel, creative ideas.

Luckily, not everyone is equally susceptible to the creative cliff illusion. In another study from the same series of experiments, we asked participants to report how frequently they engaged in creative work in their daily lives. We found that people who reported doing this kind of work more frequently were less likely to assume that creativity declined with time. Our finding suggests that personal experience with creative tasks can help people overcome their flawed assumptions about the creative process. In a third study, we found that regardless of past experience, simply telling people about this illusion can help to attenuate it.

Given these findings, there are a few things that managers can do to help their teams reset their expectations about the creative process and empower people to develop more creative ideas.

Educating Your People

Our research showed how pervasive the creative cliff illusion is—but it also illustrated that a better understanding of the phenomenon can reduce its potency. Managers should educate their teams about this illusion, explaining that a person's first ideas are unlikely to be as valuable as those that emerge later in the process. A manager can have one-on-one conversations with key employees or conduct teamwide discussions about how project workflows could be adapted to overcome this first-ideas bias.

In addition, managers can remind people that when their productivity declines and they begin to feel as if they're running out of ideas, this feeling doesn't mean that they are running low on creativity. While this sense of ineffectuality may be uncomfortable, it is actually the mind pushing its cognitive boundaries and searching for novel connections—two key conditions for generating creative ideas.

Investing in Your Creative Process

There is no set formula for success (such as "committing X% more time to the ideation process will give you Y% more creative ideas"). But there are several ways to ensure you're giving key creative processes the time and attention they need:

- Set aside more time for creative processes than you might think is necessary—whether that means an extra ideation session, a longer brainstorm, or even dedicated buffer time that can be used for additional meetings if needed.

- Ask your team to generate two or even three times as many ideas as you think you need, particularly in the early stages of ideation. Setting aggressive idea quotas can help people push past more obvious, early-stage ideas and uncover truly novel opportunities.

- Experiment with your team's creative processes, and measure the results. You can then use that data to drive future decisions. For example, the next time you run a workshop, track when the best ideas were generated. Did they come from the team that brainstormed for one hour or the team that took three hours? Did increasing your team's idea quota produce more highly creative proposals? Testing these different variables can help you calibrate your process and capture your team's creative potential.

The creative cliff illusion is very common—but it's also something that managers can help their teams overcome through a combination of education and process improvements. With the strategies outlined here, leaders can help their people understand how creativity works and build a process that emphasizes the value of late-stage ideas. Although it may take some extra work, the effort will be rewarded when you reach the potentially game-changing ideas that are uncovered through a lengthier ideation process.

Loran Nordgren is a professor of management and organizations at the Kellogg School of Management. **Brian Lucas** is an assistant professor at the Industrial and Labor Relations School, Cornell University.

Make Your Organization More Creative

CHAPTER 21

The Business Case for Curiosity

by Francesca Gino

Most of the breakthrough discoveries and remarkable inventions throughout history, from flints for starting a fire to self-driving cars, have something in common: They are the result of curiosity. The impulse to seek new information and experiences and explore novel possibilities is a basic human attribute. New research points to three important insights about curiosity as it relates to business.

First, curiosity is much more important to an enterprise's performance than was previously thought. That's because cultivating it at all levels helps leaders and their employees adapt to uncertain market conditions and

Adapted from an article in *Harvard Business Review*, September–October 2018 (product #S18051).

external pressures: When our curiosity is triggered, we think more deeply and rationally about decisions and come up with more-creative solutions. In addition, curiosity allows leaders to gain more respect from their followers and inspires employees to make their relationships with colleagues even more trusting and more collaborative.

Second, by making small changes to the design of their organizations and the ways they manage their employees, leaders can encourage curiosity—and improve their companies. These advantages accrue in every industry and in creative and routine work alike.

Third, although leaders might say they treasure inquisitive minds, in fact most stifle curiosity, fearing it will increase risk and inefficiency. In a survey I conducted of more than 3,000 employees from a wide range of firms and industries, only about 24% reported regularly feeling curious in their jobs, and about 70% said they face barriers to asking more questions at work.

In this chapter, I'll elaborate on the benefits of, and common barriers to, curiosity in the workplace. I'll then offer five strategies that can help leaders get high returns on investments in employees' curiosity and in their own.

The Benefits of Curiosity

New research reveals a wide range of benefits for organizations, leaders, and employees.

Fewer decision-making errors

In my research, I found that when our curiosity is triggered, we are less likely to fall prey to confirmation bias (looking for information that supports our beliefs rather than for evidence suggesting we are wrong) and to stereotyping people (making broad judgments, such as that women or minorities don't make good leaders). Curiosity has these positive effects because it leads us to generate alternatives.

More innovation and positive changes in both creative and noncreative jobs

Consider this example: In a field study, INSEAD's Spencer Harrison and colleagues asked artisans selling their goods through an e-commerce website several questions aimed at assessing the curiosity they experience at work. After that, the participants' creativity was measured by the number of items they created and listed over a two-week period. A one-unit increase in curiosity (for instance, a score of 6 rather than 5 on a 7-point scale) was associated with 34% greater creativity.

In a separate study, Harrison and his colleagues focused on call centers, where jobs tend to be highly structured and turnover is generally high. They asked incoming hires at 10 organizations to complete a survey that, among other things, measured their curiosity before they began their new jobs. Four weeks in, the employees were surveyed about various aspects of their work. The results showed that the most curious employees sought the most information from coworkers, and the information helped them in their jobs—for instance, it boosted their creativity in addressing customers' concerns.

My own research confirms that encouraging people to be curious generates workplace improvements. For one study, I recruited about 200 employees working in various companies and industries. Twice a week for four weeks, half of them received a text message at the start of their workday that read, "What is one topic or activity you are curious about today? What is one thing you usually take for granted that you want to ask about? Please make sure you ask a few 'Why questions' as you engage in your work throughout the day. Please set aside a few minutes to identify how you'll approach your work today with these questions in mind."

The other half (the control group) received a message designed to trigger reflection but not raise their curiosity: "What is one topic or activity you'll engage in today? What is one thing you usually work on or do that you'll also complete today? Please make sure you think about this as you engage in your work throughout the day. Please set aside a few minutes to identify how you'll approach your work today with these questions in mind."

After four weeks, the participants in the first group scored higher than the others did on questions assessing their innovative behaviors at work, such as whether they had made constructive suggestions for implementing solutions to pressing organizational problems.

When we are curious, we view tough situations more creatively. Studies have found that curiosity is associated with less defensive reactions to stress and less aggressive reactions to provocation. We also perform better when we're curious. In a study of 120 employees, I found that natural curiosity was associated with better job performance, as evaluated by their direct bosses.

Reduced group conflict

My research shows that curiosity encourages members of a group to put themselves in one another's shoes and take an interest in one another's ideas rather than focus only on their own perspective. This outward focus causes people to work together more effectively and smoothly: Conflicts are less heated, and groups achieve better results.

More-open communication and better team performance

Working with executives in a leadership program at Harvard Kennedy School, my colleagues and I divided a group of participants into smaller groups of five or six. We had some groups participate in a task that heightened their curiosity, and then we asked all the groups to engage in a simulation that tracked performance. The groups whose curiosity had been heightened performed better than did the control groups, because the curious groups shared information more openly and listened more carefully.

Barriers to Curiosity

Despite the well-established benefits of curiosity, organizations often discourage it. This attitude is not because leaders don't see the value of curiosity. On the contrary, both leaders and employees understand that curiosity creates positive outcomes for their companies. In the previously mentioned survey of more than 3,000 employees, 92% credited curious people with bringing new ideas into teams and organizations and viewed curiosity as a catalyst for job satisfaction, motivation, innovation, and high performance.

Yet executives' actions often tell a different story. True, some organizations, including 3M and Meta (formerly Facebook), give employees free time to pursue their interests, but these companies are rare. And even in such organizations, employees often have challenging short-term performance goals (such as meeting a quarterly sales target or launching a new product by a certain date). These goals tend to consume the free time people could have spent exploring alternative approaches to their work or coming up with innovative ideas.

Two tendencies restrain leaders from encouraging curiosity.

They have the wrong mindset about exploration

Leaders often think that letting employees follow their curiosity will lead to a costly mess. In a recent survey of 520 chief learning officers and chief talent development officers, I found that they often shy away from encouraging curiosity because they believe the company would be harder to manage if people were allowed to explore their own interests. They also believe that disagreements would arise and that making and executing decisions would slow down, raising the cost of doing business.

Research finds that although people list creativity as a goal, they frequently reject creative ideas when actually presented with them. That's understandable: Exploration often involves questioning the status quo and doesn't always produce useful information. But it also means not settling for the first possible solution—and so creative exploration often yields better remedies.

They seek efficiency to the detriment of exploration

In the early 1900s, Henry Ford focused all his efforts on one goal: reducing production costs to create a car for the masses. By 1908, he had realized that vision with the introduction of the Model T. Demand grew so high that by 1921, the company was producing 56% of all passenger cars in the United States—a remarkable success made possible primarily by the firm's efficiency-centered model of work. But in the late 1920s, as the U.S. economy rose to new heights, consumers started wanting greater variety in their cars. While Ford remained fixated on improving the Model T, competitors such as General Motors started producing an array of models and soon captured the main share of the market. Owing to its single-minded focus on efficiency, Ford stopped experimenting and innovating and fell behind.

These leadership tendencies help explain why our curiosity usually declines the longer we're in a job. In one survey, I asked about 250 people who had recently started working for various companies a series of questions designed to measure curiosity; six months later, I administered a follow-up survey. Although initial levels of curiosity varied, everyone's curiosity had dropped after six months, with the average decline exceeding 20%. Because people were under pressure to complete their work quickly, they had little time to ask questions about broad processes or overall goals.

Five Ways to Bolster Curiosity

It takes thought and discipline to stop stifling curiosity and start fostering it. Here are five strategies leaders can employ.

Hire for curiosity

In 2004, an anonymous billboard appeared on Highway 101, in the heart of Silicon Valley, posing this puzzle: "{first 10-digit prime found in consecutive digits of e}.com." The answer, 7427466391.com, led the curious online, where they found another equation to solve. The handful of people who did so were invited to submit a résumé to Google. The company took this unusual approach to finding job candidates because it places a premium on curiosity. (People didn't even need to be engineers!) As Eric Schmidt, Google's CEO from 2001 to 2011, has said, "We run this company on questions, not answers."

Google also identifies naturally curious people through interview questions such as these: "Have you ever found yourself unable to stop learning something you've never encountered before? Why? What kept you persistent?" The answers usually highlight either a specific purpose driving the candidate's inquiry ("It was my job to find the answer") or genuine curiosity ("I just had to figure out the answer").

IDEO, a design and consulting company, seeks to hire "T-shaped" employees. These people have deep skills that allow them to contribute to the creative process (the vertical stroke of the T) and a predisposition for collaboration across disciplines, a quality requiring empathy and curiosity (the horizontal stroke of the T). The firm understands that empathy and curiosity are related: Empathy allows employees to listen thoughtfully and see problems or decisions from another person's perspective, while curiosity extends to interest in other people's disciplines, so much so that one may start to practice them. And IDEO recognizes that most people perform at their best not because they're specialists but because their deep skill is accompanied by an intellectual curiosity that leads them to ask questions, explore, and collaborate.

To identify potential employees who are T-shaped, IDEO pays attention to how candidates talk about past projects. People who focus only on their own contributions may lack the breadth to appreciate collaboration. T-shaped candidates are more likely to talk about how they succeeded with the help of others and to express interest in working collaboratively on future projects.

To assess curiosity, employers can also ask candidates about their interests outside work. Reading books unrelated to one's own field and exploring questions just for the sake of knowing the answers are indications of curiosity. And companies can administer curiosity assessments, which have been validated in a myriad of studies. These tests generally measure whether people explore things they don't know, analyze data to uncover new ideas, read widely beyond their field, have diverse interests outside work, and are excited by learning opportunities.

The questions candidates ask—not just the answers they provide—can also signal curiosity. For instance, people who want to know about organizational aspects that aren't directly related to the job at hand probably have more natural curiosity than do people who ask only about the role they would perform.

Model inquisitiveness

Leaders can encourage curiosity throughout their organizations by being inquisitive themselves. In 2000, when Greg Dyke had been named director general of the BBC but hadn't yet assumed the position, he spent five months visiting the BBC's major locations, assembling the staff at each stop. Employees expected a long presentation but instead got a simple question: "What is the one thing I should do to make things better for you?" Dyke would listen carefully and then ask, "What is the one thing I should do to make things better for our viewers and listeners?"

The BBC's employees respected their new boss for taking the time to ask questions and listen. Dyke used their responses to inform his thinking about the changes needed to solve problems facing the broadcaster and to identify what to work on first. After officially taking the reins, he addressed the staff in a speech that reflected what he had learned and showed that he had been truly interested in what they said.

By asking questions and genuinely listening to the responses, Dyke modeled the importance of those behaviors. He also highlighted the fact that when we are exploring new terrain, listening is as important as talking:

It helps us fill gaps in our knowledge and identify other questions to investigate.

The importance of listening may seem intuitive, but my research shows that we often prefer talking over listening with curiosity. For instance, when I asked some 230 high-level leaders in executive education classes what they would do if confronted with an organizational crisis stemming from both financial and cultural issues, most said they would take action: move to stop the financial bleeding and introduce initiatives to refresh the culture. Only a few said they would ask questions rather than simply impose their ideas on others. Management books commonly encourage leaders assuming new positions to communicate their vision from the start instead of asking employees how they can be most helpful. It's bad advice.

Why do we refrain from asking questions? Because we fear we'll be judged incompetent, indecisive, or unintelligent. Plus, time is precious, and we don't want to bother people. Experience and expertise exacerbate the problem: As people climb the organizational ladder, they think they have less to learn. Leaders also tend to believe they're expected to talk and provide answers, not ask questions.

Such fears and beliefs are misplaced, my recent research shows. When we demonstrate curiosity about others by asking questions, people like us *more* and view us as *more* competent, and the heightened trust makes our relationships more interesting and intimate. By asking questions, we promote more-meaningful connections and more-creative outcomes.

Leaders can also model curiosity by acknowledging when they don't know the answer; admitting the limits of your knowledge makes it clear that it's OK to be guided by curiosity. Patricia Fili-Krushel told me that when she joined WebMD Health as CEO, she met with a group of male engineers in Silicon Valley. They were doubtful that she could add value to their work and, right off the bat, asked what she knew about engineering. Without hesitation, Fili-Krushel made a zero with her fingers. "This is how much I know about engineering," she told them. "However, I do know how to run businesses, and I'm hoping you can teach me what I need to know about your world." When leaders concede that they don't have the answer to a question, they show that they value the search for answers and motivate others to explore as well.

New hires at Pixar Animation Studios are often hesitant to question the status quo, given the company's track record of hit movies and the brilliant work of those who have been there for years. To combat that tendency, Ed Catmull, the cofounder and president, makes a point of talking about times when Pixar made bad choices. Like all other organizations, he says, Pixar is not perfect, and it needs fresh eyes to spot opportunities for improvement. In this way, Catmull gives new recruits license to question existing practices. Recognizing the limits of our own knowledge and skills sends a powerful signal to others.

Tenelle Porter, a postdoctoral scholar in psychology at the University of California, Davis, describes intellectual humility as the ability to acknowledge that what we know is sharply limited. As her research demonstrates, higher levels of intellectual humility are associated with a greater willingness to consider views other than our own. People with more intellectual humility also do better in school and at work. Why? When we accept that our own knowledge is finite, we are more apt to see that the world is always changing and that the future will diverge from the present. By embracing this insight, leaders and employees can begin to recognize the power of exploration.

Finally, leaders can model inquisitiveness by approaching the unknown with curiosity rather than judgment. Bob Langer, who heads one of MIT's most productive laboratories, told me recently that this principle guides how he manages his staff. As human beings, we all feel an urge to evaluate others—often not positively. We're quick to judge their ideas, behaviors, and perspectives, even when they relate to things that haven't been tried before. Langer avoids this trap by raising questions about others' ideas. His curiosity leads people to think deeper about their perspective and to remain curious about the tough problems they are trying to tackle. Through his thoughtful questions, he is modeling behavior that he expects of others in the lab.

Emphasize learning goals

When I asked Captain Chesley "Sully" Sullenberger how he was able to land a commercial aircraft safely in the Hudson River, he described his passion for continuous learning. Although commercial flights are almost always routine, every time his plane pushed back from the gate, he would remind himself that he needed to be prepared for the unexpected. "What can I learn?" he would think. When the unexpected came to pass, on a cold January day in 2009, Sullenberger asked himself what he *could* do, given the available options, and came up with a creative solution. He successfully fought the tendency to grasp for the most obvious option (landing at the nearest airport). Especially when under pressure, we narrow in on what immediately seems the best course of action. But those who are passionate about continuous learning contemplate a wide range of options and perspectives. As the accident report shows, Sullenberger carefully considered several alternatives in the 208 seconds between his discovery that the aircraft's engines lacked thrust and his landing of the plane in the Hudson.

It's natural to concentrate on results, especially in the face of tough challenges. But focusing on learning is generally more beneficial to people and their organizations, as some landmark studies show. For example, when U.S. Air Force personnel were given a demanding goal for the number of planes to be landed in a set time, their performance *decreased*. Similarly, in a study led by Southern Methodist University's Don Vandewalle, sales professionals who were naturally focused on performance goals, such as meeting their targets and being seen by colleagues as good at their jobs, did worse during a promotion of a product (a piece of medical equipment priced at about $5,400) than did reps who were naturally focused on learning goals, such as exploring how to be a better salesperson. The results orientation cost these salespeople, because the company awarded a bonus of $300 for each unit sold.

A body of research demonstrates that framing work around learning goals (developing competence, acquiring skills, mastering new situations, and so on) rather than performance goals (hitting targets, proving our competence, impressing others) boosts motivation. And when motivated by learning goals, we acquire a more diverse set of skills, do better at work, get higher grades in college, do better in problem-solving, and receive higher ratings after training. Unfortunately, organizations often prioritize performance goals.

Leaders can help employees adopt a learning mindset by communicating the importance of learning and by rewarding people not only for their performance but also for the learning needed to get there. Deloitte took this path: In 2013, it replaced its performance management system with one that tracks both learning and performance. Employees meet regularly with a coach to discuss their development and learning along with the support they need to continually grow.

Leaders can also stress the value of learning by reacting positively to ideas that may be mediocre in themselves but could be springboards to better ones. Writers and directors at Pixar are trained in a technique called *plussing*, which involves building on ideas without using judgmental language. Instead of rejecting a sketch, for example, a director might find a starting point by saying, "I like Woody's eyes, and what if we . . . ?" Someone else might jump in with another plus. This technique allows people to remain curious, listen actively, respect the ideas of others, and contribute their own. By promoting a process that allows all sorts of ideas to be explored, leaders send a clear message that learning is a key goal even if it doesn't always lead to success.

Let employees explore and broaden their interests

Organizations can foster curiosity by giving employees time and resources to explore their interests. One of my favorite examples comes from my native country. It involves Italy's first typewriter factory, Olivetti, founded in 1908 in the foothills of the Italian Alps. In the 1930s, some employees caught a coworker leaving the factory with a bagful of iron pieces and machinery. They accused him of stealing and asked the company to fire him. The worker told the CEO, Adriano Olivetti, that he was taking the parts home to work on a new machine over the weekend because he didn't have time while performing his regular job. Instead of firing him, Olivetti gave him time to create the machine and charged him with overseeing its production. The result was Divisumma, the first electronic calculator. Divisumma sold well worldwide in the 1950s and 1960s, and Olivetti promoted the worker to technical director. Unlike leaders who would have shown him the door, Olivetti gave him the space to explore his curiosity, with remarkable results.

Some organizations provide resources to support employees' outside interests. Since 1996, the manufacturing conglomerate United Technologies (UTC) has given as much as $12,000 in tuition annually to any employee seeking a degree part-time—no strings attached. Leaders often don't want to invest in training employees, for fear that the worker will jump to a competitor and take their expensively acquired skills with them. Even though UTC hasn't tried to quantify the benefits of its tuition reimbursement program, Gail Jackson, the vice president of human resources when we spoke, believes in the importance of curious employees. "It's better to train and have them leave than not to train and have them stay," she told me. But according to the Society for Human Resource Management's 2017 employee benefits report, only 44% of organizations provide or support cross-training to develop skills not directly related to workers' jobs.

Leaders might provide opportunities for employees to travel to unfamiliar locales. When we have chances to expand our interests, research has found, we not only remain curious but also become more confident about what we can accomplish and we grow more successful at work. Employees can "travel" to other roles and areas of the organization to gain a broader perspective. At Pixar, employees across the organization can provide "notes"—questions and advice—that help directors consider all sorts of possibilities for the movies they are working on.

Employees can also broaden their interests by expanding their networks. As I and my colleagues Tiziana Casciaro, Bill McEvily, and Evelyn Zhang have found, curious people often end up being star performers, thanks to their diverse networks. Because they're more comfortable than others are with asking questions, curious people more easily create and nurture ties at work— and those ties are critical to their career development and success. The organization benefits when employees are connected to people who can help them with challenges and motivate them to go the extra mile. MIT's Bob Langer works to raise curiosity in his students by introducing them to experts in his network. Similarly, by connecting people across organizational departments and units, leaders can encourage employees to be curious about their colleagues' work and ways of doing business.

Deliberate thinking about workspaces can broaden networks and encourage the cross-pollination of ideas. In the 1990s, when Pixar was designing a new home for itself in Emeryville, California, across the bay from San Francisco, the initial plans called for a separate building for each department. But then-owner Steve Jobs had concerns about isolating the various departments and decided to build a single structure with a large atrium in the center, containing employee mailboxes, a café, a gift shop, and screening rooms. Forcing employees to interact, he reasoned, would expose them to one another's work and ideas.

Leaders can also boost employees' curiosity by carefully designing their teams. Consider Massimo Bottura, the owner of Osteria Francescana, a three-Michelin-star restaurant in Modena, Italy, that was rated the Best Restaurant in the World in 2016 and 2018. His sous chefs are Davide di Fabio, from Italy, and Kondo Takahiko, from Japan. The two differ not only in their origins but also in their strengths: Di Fabio is more comfortable with improvisation, while Takahiko is obsessed with precision. Such collisions of these two approaches make the kitchen more innovative, Bottura believes, and inspire curiosity in other workers.

Have "Why?" "What if?" and "How might we?" days

The inspiration for the Polaroid instant camera was a three-year-old's question. Inventor Edwin Land's daughter was impatient to see a photo her father had just snapped. When he explained that the film had to be processed, she wondered aloud, "Why do we have to wait for the picture?"

As every parent knows, *why* is ubiquitous in the vocabulary of young children, who have an insatiable need to understand the world around them. They aren't afraid to ask questions, and they don't worry about whether others believe they should already know the answers. But as children grow older, self-consciousness creeps in, along with the desire to appear confident and demonstrate expertise. By the time we're adults, we often suppress our curiosity.

Leaders can help draw out our innate curiosity. One company I visited asked all employees to think about and articulate some "What if?" and "How might we?" questions about the firm's goals and plans. They came up with all sorts of things, which were discussed and evaluated. As a concrete sign that questioning was supported and rewarded, the best questions were displayed on banners hung on the walls. Some of the questions led employees to suggest ideas for how to work more effectively. (For more on the importance of asking good questions before seeking solutions, see chapter 9.)

In one study, my colleagues and I asked adults working in a wide range of jobs and industries to read about three organizational elements: goals, roles, and how organizations as a whole work together. For half the workers, the information was presented as the *grow method*—our version of a control condition. We encouraged that group to view those elements as immutable, and we stressed the importance of following existing processes that managers had already defined. For the other half, the information was presented as the *go-back method*. We encouraged those employees to see the elements as fluid and to go back and rethink them. A week later, we found that the workers who had read about the go-back method showed more creativity in tasks than did the workers in the grow-method group. They were more open to others' ideas and worked more effectively with one another.

To encourage curiosity, leaders should also teach employees how to ask good questions. Langer has said he wants to "help people make the transition from giving good answers to asking good questions." He also tells his students that they could change the world, thus boosting the curiosity they need to tackle challenging problems.

Organizing "Why?" days, when employees are encouraged to ask that question if facing a challenge, can go a long way toward fostering curiosity. Intellectual Ventures, a company that generates inventions and buys and licenses patents, organizes "invention sessions" in which people from different disciplines, backgrounds, and levels of expertise come together to discuss potential solutions to tough problems. The diversity of participants helps them consider issues from various angles. Similarly, under Toyota's five-whys approach, employees are encouraged to investigate problems by asking why. After coming up with an answer, they are supposed to ask why this answer is the case, and so on, until they have asked the question five times. This mindset can help employees innovate by challenging their existing perspectives.

In most organizations, leaders and employees alike receive the implicit message that asking questions is an unwanted challenge to authority. They are trained to focus on their work without looking closely at the process or their overall goals. But maintaining a sense of wonder is crucial to creativity and innovation. The most effective leaders look for ways to nurture their employees' curiosity to fuel learning and discovery.

———————

Francesca Gino is a behavioral scientist and the Tandon Family Professor of Business Administration at Harvard Business School. She is the author of the books *Rebel Talent: Why It Pays to Break the Rules at Work and in Life* and *Sidetracked: Why Our Decisions Get Derailed, and How We Can Stick to the Plan.*

CHAPTER 22

How Leaders Can Unlock Their Teams' Creativity

by Rebecca Shambaugh

As a leadership coach, I never miss an opportunity to ask senior-level executives what they see as critical for people and organizations to succeed in today's dynamic business environment. A while ago, I met with an executive vice president of a *Fortune* 500 company. This executive (let's call her Ashley) has built many national and global teams and serves as a highly inspirational leader for her organization and industry. Without reservation, Ashley told me that being creative and innovative are the

---

Adapted from "How to Unlock Your Team's Creativity" on hbr.org, January 31, 2019 (product #H04RQ5).

top critical success factors—not only for companies but also for leaders and their teams. Research has validated these findings, identifying creativity as the top leadership competency for enterprises.

Ashley explained that leaders and managers can't continue to rely on the same ideas that have brought them past success. Nor can they be effective by surrounding themselves with people who parrot the leader's own ideas. "I don't want the people who work for me to just take orders or feed information to me," she said. "I encourage my teams to take risks in bringing fresh thinking and new ideas to the table, even if they are not one hundred percent correct." Ashley added that the complexities of today's marketplace require innovative solutions, which at times call for disruptive ways of problem-solving—ways that may challenge the status quo: "The business environment is too dynamic, and the level of change is too complex. We can't rely on the same ideas or same ways to solve problems or expand markets with the same thinking we've always fallen back on."

With this understanding, Ashley looks for talent that puts thought into novel ways to address an issue or make a decision, rather than someone who operates in a vacuum of expected solutions. She believes that leaders must ensure not only that they have the right talent on their teams but also that those teams can thrive. To this end, she wants leaders to create an environment that encourages innovative thinking and that inspires people to tap into, and share, their best ideas and limitless creative potential. But how can leaders achieve Ashley's vision to unleash the full range of top thinking in their teams? Here are some strategies to get any group's creative juices flowing.

Avoid getting hemmed in by process

Innovation is driven neither by processes nor systems; it's generated by human talent. No matter what procedures you have in place, only the creative confidence and drive of individuals—and the collective intelligence of teams—will take companies to new frontiers, revealing a better world and boosting an organization's bottom-line performance.

If a team is creatively blocked, a first step for leadership is to examine whether the processes that surround people are holding them hostage in their thinking. An overreliance on systematically following rules can shut down collaborative brainstorming, as some people may believe they have no flexibility to express outside options that run counter to the standard process—the way that things have always been done. If this is the case, try removing the limitations of particular procedural structures during your creative sessions so that everyone can feel freer to contribute without bureaucratic constraint.

Facilitate spaghetti throwing

In my work with client companies, I've observed firsthand that teams truly empowered to exercise their creativity are purposeful, engaged, and inspired to do great things. They find ways to make life better for customers. Since this is the goal of every competitive organization, today's leaders must provide the right environment for teams to tap into their full range of creative thinking and ability. While research shows that 80% of people see unlocking creative potential as key to economic growth, only 25% think they are living up to their own creative potential. From the employer side, McKinsey & Company's research has revealed that an overwhelming majority of executives—94%—are unhappy with the innovative performance of their company. That's a huge waste of talent in an area where leaders can make a major impact simply by allowing the work environment to be more conducive to creative contributions.

To facilitate experimentation and encourage people to see what sticks and what doesn't, work on creating an environment of psychological safety—where Heidi Brooks from the Yale School of Management says, a leader "walks the talk and doesn't simply ask people to voice outside-the-box thinking, but also demonstrates the same behaviors himself or herself." To inspire creativity, leaders should also encourage healthy conflict and debate. Instead of micromanaging, empower others and give them the reins to explore and take risks. Doing so can lead a group in unexpected directions. (For more on psychological safety on creative teams, see chapter 17.)

Reveal "sticky floors"

Everyone has the foundation to become creative. They start with the belief that they themselves are idea generators with the ability to become a compelling voice for creative concepts. When someone on the team harbors the opposite belief—that they aren't inherently innovative—their self-assessment can quickly become what I refer to as a *sticky floor*: a self-limiting belief or assumption that can sabotage success.

As a leader, part of your role in managing teams is to use emotional intelligence to determine whether any team members are unknowingly holding themselves back from tapping into their talents and full potential. If even one person hides their creative light under a bushel, the whole team suffers. Take a proactive approach to address this issue: Help the team member see the sticky floor, and offer coaching and support to help them express innovative ideas in the team setting.

Encourage a growth mindset—one laced with mindfulness

As part of coaching team members off their sticky floors, you'll want to help them understand how to develop a growth mindset. The term *growth mindset*, coined by Stanford University professor Carol Dweck, refers to how a person thinks about their own abilities related to intelligence and learning. People with a growth mindset possess an underlying belief that they can improve through their own effort. They accept setbacks and don't see them as failures but rather see them as opportunities for growing and learning through a process of gradual improvement. This perspective is the counterpoint to a *fixed mindset*, in which people believe they have a set level of talent (or lack thereof) in a particular area and that they can't alter that level, no matter how hard they try. When team members encounter a sticky floor related to creativity, leaders should coach them, explaining how the internal belief that they can become more creative helps them continue to develop their skills over time, learning from their mistakes and making improvements. In short, developing a growth mindset is about helping people move from fear to courage, and from perfectionism to a level of excellence that's "good enough." This leadership challenge calls for guiding people to step out of the norm, crack their old assumptions, and stay open to new possibilities for creative insights.

Studies suggest that a mindfulness practice can help teams amplify the results of a growth mindset by courting creativity. Many of today's leaders have lost their ability and the bandwidth to pause and prioritize what's important or to put time aside to plan and be creative while inspiring others to do the same. Yet this omission is a mistake, in light of research that reveals that meditation awakens creative impulses in several ways, such as by improving working memory, cognitive flexibility, and brainstorming ability. Increasing mindfulness can be as simple as taking a walk in the middle of the day while focusing on your surroundings. Avoid the tendency to multitask. Get rid of tech distractions at set times for freeform thought, and do a simple breathing exercise, following the rise and fall of your breath to oxygenate your brain and ignite creativity. If the simple act of pausing to breathe and reflect can drive a whole team's creativity, then it's a step worth implementing.

The goal of getting your team to think beyond the box is a no-brainer, but figuring out how to actually achieve greater group innovation isn't. As a leader, you need to approach making this happen just as you would any other management challenge: creatively.

———————

Rebecca Shambaugh is an internationally recognized leadership expert, author, and keynote speaker. She's President of SHAMBAUGH, a global leadership development organization, and founder of Women in Leadership and Learning.

CHAPTER 23

Build a Culture of Originality

by Adam Grant

If there's one place on earth where originality goes to die, I'd managed to find it. I was charged with unleashing innovation and change in the ultimate bastion of bureaucracy. It was a place where people accepted defaults without question, followed rules without explanation, and clung to traditions and technologies long after they'd become obsolete: the U.S. Navy.

But in a matter of months, the navy was exploding with originality—and not because of anything I'd done. It launched a major innovation task force and helped form a Department of Defense outpost in Silicon Valley

---

Adapted from "How to Build a Culture of Originality" in *Harvard Business Review*, March 2016 (product #R1603H).

to get up to speed on cutting-edge technology. Surprisingly, these changes didn't come from the top of the navy's command-and-control structure. They were initiated at the bottom, by a group of junior officers in their twenties and thirties.

When I started digging for more details, multiple insiders pointed to a young aviator named Ben Kohlmann. Officers called him a troublemaker, rabble-rouser, disrupter, heretic, and radical. And in direct violation of the military ethos, these were terms of endearment.

Kohlmann lit the match by creating the navy's first rapid-innovation cell—a network of original thinkers who would collaborate to question long-held assumptions and generate new ideas. To start assembling the group, he searched for people with a history of nonconformity. One recruit had been fired from a nuclear submarine for disobeying a commander's order. Another had flat-out refused to go to basic training. Others had yelled at senior flag officers and flouted chains of command by writing public blog posts to express their iconoclastic views. "They were lone wolves," Kohlmann says. "Most of them had a track record of insubordination."

Kohlmann realized, however, that to fuel and sustain innovation throughout the navy, he needed more than a few lone wolves. So while working as an instructor and a director of flight operations, he set about building a culture of nonconformity. He talked to senior leaders about expanding his network and got their buy-in. He recruited sailors who had never shown a desire to challenge the status quo and exposed them to new ways of thinking. They visited centers of innovation excellence outside the military, including Google and the Rocky Mountain Institute. They devoured a monthly syllabus of readings on innovation and debated ideas during regular happy hours and robust online discussions. Soon they pioneered the use of 3D printers on ships and a robotic fish for stealth underwater missions—and other rapid-innovation cells began springing up around the military. "Culture is king," Kohlmann says. "When people discovered their voice, they became unstoppable."

Empowering the rank and file to innovate is where most leaders fall short. Instead, they try to recruit brash entrepreneurial types to bring fresh ideas and energy into their organizations—and then leave it at that. It's a wrongheaded approach, because it assumes that the best innovators are rare creatures with special gifts. Research shows that entrepreneurs who succeed over the long haul are surprisingly more risk-averse than their peers. The hotshots burn bright for a while but tend to fizzle out. So relying on a few exceptional folks who fit a romanticized creative profile is a short-term move that underestimates everyone else. Most people are in fact quite capable of novel thinking and problem-solving, if only their organizations would stop pounding them into conformity.

When everyone thinks alike and sticks to dominant norms, businesses are doomed to stagnate. To fight that inertia and drive innovation and change effectively, leaders need sustained original thinking in their organizations. They get it by building a culture of nonconformity, as Kohlmann did in the navy. I've been studying this for the better part of a decade, and it turns out to be less difficult than I expected.

For starters, leaders must give employees opportunities and incentives to generate—and keep generating—new ideas so that people across functions and roles get better at pushing past the obvious. However, it's also critical to have the right people vetting those ideas. That part of the process should be much less democratic and more meritocratic, because some votes are simply more meaningful than others. And finally, to continue generating and selecting smart ideas over time, organizations need to strike a balance between cultural cohesion and creative dissent.

Letting a Thousand Flowers Bloom

People often believe that to do better work, they should do fewer things. Yet the evidence flies in the face of that assumption: Being prolific actually increases originality, because sheer volume improves your chances of finding novel solutions. In experiments by Northwestern University psychologists Brian Lucas and Loran Nordgren, the initial ideas people generated were the most conventional. Once they had thought of those, they were free to start dreaming up possibilities that were more unusual. Their first 20 ideas were significantly less original than their next 15 were. (See chapter 20 of this guide for more on creative persistence.)

Across fields, volume begets quality. This observation holds for all kinds of creators and thinkers—from composers and painters to scientists and inventors. Even the most eminent innovators do their most original work when they're also cranking out scores of less brilliant ideas. Consider Thomas Edison. In a five-year period, he came up with the light bulb, the phonograph, and the carbon transmitter used in telephones—while also filing more than 100 patents for inventions that didn't catch the world on fire, including a talking doll that ended up scaring children (and adults).

Of course, in organizations, the challenge lies in knowing when you've drummed up enough possibilities. How many ideas should you generate before deciding which ones to pursue? When I pose this question to executives, most say you're really humming with around 20 ideas. But that answer is off the mark by an order of magnitude. There's evidence that quality often doesn't max out until more than 200 ideas are on the table.

Stanford professor Robert Sutton notes that the Pixar movie *Cars* was chosen from about 500 pitches, and at Skyline, the toy design studio that generates ideas for Fisher-Price and Mattel, employees submitted 4,000 new toy concepts in one year. That group was winnowed down to 230 to be drawn or prototyped, and just 12 were finally developed. The more darts you throw, the better your odds of hitting a bull's-eye.

Though the idea that volume ultimately creates quality makes perfect sense, many managers fail to embrace this principle, fearing that time spent conjuring lots of ideas will prevent employees from being focused and efficient. The good news is that there are ways to help employees generate quantity and variety without sacrificing day-to-day productivity or causing burnout.

Think like the enemy

Research suggests that organizations often get stuck in a rut because they're playing defense, trying to stave off the competition. To encourage people to think differently and generate more ideas, put them on offense.

That's what Lisa Bodell of FutureThink did when Merck CEO Kenneth Frazier hired her to help shake up the status quo. Bodell divided Merck's executives into groups and asked them to come up with ways to put the company out of business. Instead of being cautious and sticking close to established competencies, the executives started considering bold new directions in strategy and product development—directions that competitors could conceivably take. The energy in the room soared as they explored the possibilities. The offensive mindset, Carnegie Mellon University professor Anita Woolley observes in an *Organizational Science* article, focuses attention on "pursuing opportunities . . . whereas defenders are more focused on maintaining their market share." That mental shift allowed the Merck executives to imagine competitive threats that didn't yet exist. The result was a fresh set of opportunities for innovation.

Solicit ideas from individuals, not groups

According to decades of research, you get more and better ideas if people are working alone in separate rooms than if they're brainstorming in a group. When people generate ideas together, many of the best ones never get shared. Some members dominate the conversation, others hold back to avoid looking foolish, and the whole group tends to conform to the majority's taste.

Evidence shows that these problems can be managed through *brainwriting*. All that's required is asking individuals to think up ideas on their own before the group evaluates them, to get all the possibilities on the table. For instance, at the eyewear retailer Warby Parker, named the world's most innovative company by *Fast Company* in 2015, employees spend a few minutes a week writing down innovation ideas for colleagues to read and comment on. The company also maintains a Google doc where employees can submit requests for new technology to be built. The document yields about 400 new ideas in a typical quarter. One major innovation was a revamped retail point of sale, which grew out of an app that allowed customers to bookmark their favorite frames in the store and receive an email about them later.

Since employees often withhold their most unusual suggestions in group settings, another strategy for seeking ideas is to schedule rapid one-on-one idea meetings. When Anita Krohn Traaseth became managing director of Hewlett-Packard Norway, she launched a "speed-date the boss" initiative. She invited every employee to meet with her for five minutes and answer these questions: Who are you, and what do you do at HP? Where do you think we should change, and what should we keep focusing on? And what do you want to contribute beyond fulfilling your job responsibilities? She made it clear that she expected people to bring big ideas, and they didn't want to waste their five minutes with a senior leader—it was their chance to show that they could innovate. More than 170 speed dates later, so many good ideas had been generated that other HP leaders implemented the process in Austria and Switzerland.

Bring back the suggestion box

It's a practice that dates back to the early 1700s, when a Japanese shogun put a box at the entrance to his castle. He rewarded good ideas—but punished criticisms with decapitation. Today suggestion boxes are often ridiculed. "I smell a creative idea being formed somewhere in the building," the boss thinks in one *Dilbert* cartoon. "I must find it and crush it." He sets up a suggestion box, and Dilbert is intrigued until a colleague warns him: "It's a trap!!"

But the evidence points to a different conclusion: Suggestion boxes can be quite useful, precisely because they provide a large number of ideas. In one study, psychologist Michael Frese and his colleagues visited a Dutch steel company (now part of Tata Steel) that had been using a suggestion program for 70 years. The company had 11,000 employees and collected between 7,000 and 12,000 suggestions a year. A typical employee would make six or seven suggestions annually and see three or four adopted. One prolific innovator submitted 75 ideas and had 30 adopted. In many companies, those ideas would have been missed altogether. For the Dutch steelmaker, however, the suggestion box regularly led to improvements—saving more than $750,000 in one year alone.

The major benefit of suggestion boxes is that they multiply and diversify the ideas on the horizon, opening up new avenues for innovation. The biggest hurdle is that they create a larger haystack of ideas, making it more difficult to find the needle. You need a system for culling contributions—and rewarding and pursuing the best ones—so that people don't feel their suggestions are falling on deaf ears.

Developing a Nose for Good Ideas

Generating lots of alternatives is important, but so is listening to the right opinions and solutions. How can leaders avoid pursuing bad ideas and rejecting good ones?

Lean on proven evaluators

Although many leaders use a democratic process to select ideas, not every vote is equally valuable. Bowing to the majority's will is not the best policy; a select minority might have a better sense of which ideas have the greatest potential. To figure out whose votes should be amplified, pay attention to employees' track records in evaluation.

At the hedge fund Bridgewater, employees' opinions are weighted by a believability score, which reflects the quality of their past decisions in that domain. In the U.S. intelligence community, analysts demonstrate their credibility by forecasting major political and economic events. In studies conducted by psychologist Philip Tetlock and described in his book *Superforecasting*, forecasters are rated on accuracy (did they make the right bets?) and calibration (did they get the probabilities right?). Once the best of these prognosticators are identified, their judgments can be given greater influence than those of their peers.

So, in a company, who is likely to have the strongest track record? Not managers—it's too easy for them to stick to existing prototypes. And not the innovators themselves. Intoxicated by their own eureka moments, they tend to be overconfident about their odds of success. They may try to compensate for that by researching customer preferences, but they'll still be susceptible to confirmation bias (looking for information that supports their view and rejecting the rest). Even creative geniuses have trouble predicting with any accuracy when they've come up with a winner.

Research suggests that fellow innovators are the best evaluators of original ideas. They're impartial, because they're not judging their own ideas, and they're more willing than managers to give radical possibilities a chance. For example, Stanford professor Justin Berg found that circus performers who evaluated videos of their peers' new acts were about twice as accurate as managers were in predicting popularity with audiences.

Make it a contest

Idea competitions can help leaders separate the wheat from the chaff, whether they're sifting through suggestion-box entries or hosting a live innovation event. At Dow Chemical Company, for example, employees participate in an annual innovation tournament focused on reducing waste and saving energy. The tournament calls for ideas that require an initial investment of no more than $200,000, and those costs must be recoverable within a year. Peers review the submissions, with monetary rewards going to the winners. Innovation researchers Christian Terwiesch and Karl Ulrich report that over more than a decade, the resulting 575 projects have produced an average return of 204% and saved the company $110 million a year.

When an innovation tournament is well designed, you get a large pool of initial ideas, but they're clustered around key themes instead of spanning a range of topics. Because people spend a lot of time preparing their entries, the quality can be good, but the work happens in a discrete window of time, so the contest is not a recurring distraction.

Thorough evaluation helps to filter out the bad ideas. The feedback process typically involves having a group of subject matter experts and fellow innovators review the submissions, rate their novelty and usefulness, and suggest improvements.

With the right judges in place, an innovation contest not only leverages the wisdom of the crowd but also makes the crowd wiser. Contributors and evaluators get to learn from other people's successes and failures. Over time, the culture can evolve into one where employees feel confident in their ability to contribute ideas—and develop a better sense of what constitutes quality. Because successful innovators earn recognition and rewards, everyone has an incentive to participate.

So start by calling for ideas to solve a problem or seize an opportunity, and then introduce a rigorous process for assessment and feedback. The most promising submissions will make it to the next round, and the eventual winners should get the staff and resources necessary to implement their ideas.

Cultivating Both Cohesion and Dissent

Building a culture of nonconformity begins with learning how to generate and vet ideas, but it doesn't end there. To maintain originality over time, leaders need to keep fighting the pressures against it.

We used to blame conformity on strong cultures, believing they were so cultish and chummy that members couldn't consider diverse views and make wise decisions. But that's not true. Studies of decision-making in top management teams show that cohesive groups are not more likely than others are to seek consensus, dismiss divergent opinions, and fall victim to groupthink. In fact, members of strong cultures often make better decisions because they communicate well with one another and are secure enough in their roles to feel comfortable challenging one another.

Here's the evidence on how successful high-tech founders in Silicon Valley built their startups: They hired primarily for commitment to the mission, looking for people who would help carry out their vision and live by their values. Founders who looked mainly for technical skill or star potential didn't fare nearly as well. In mature industries, too, studies have shown that when companies place a strong emphasis on culture, their performance remains more stable.

Yet there's a dark side to strong, cohesive cultures: They can become homogeneous if left unchecked. As leaders continue to attract, select, and retain similar people, they sacrifice diversity in thoughts and values. Employees face intense pressure to fit in or get out. This sameness can be advantageous in predictable environments, but it's a problem in volatile industries and dynamic markets. In those settings, strong cultures can be too insular to respond appropriately to shifting conditions. Leaders have a hard time recognizing the need for change, considering different views, and learning and adapting.

Consider BlackBerry: After disrupting the smartphone market, senior leaders clung to the belief that users were primarily interested in efficient, secure email. They dismissed the iPhone as a music player and a consumer toy, hired like-minded insiders who had engineering backgrounds but lacked marketing expertise, and ultimately failed to create a high-quality web browser and an app-friendly operating system. The result? A major downsizing, a billion-dollar write-off, and a colossal collapse of market share.

So to balance out a strong culture, you also need a steady supply of critical opinions. Even when they're wrong, they're useful—they disrupt knee-jerk consensus, stimulate original thought, and help organizations find novel solutions to problems. In the navy's rapid-innovation cell, the norm is "loyal opposition," says Joshua Marcuse, one of Kohlmann's collaborators in the Pentagon. "Agitating against the status quo is how we contribute to the mission."

In short, make dissent one of your organization's core values. Create an environment where people can openly share critical opinions and are respected for doing so. In the early days of Apple, employees were passionately committed to making the Mac a user-friendly household product. But each year, the Mac team also gave an award to somebody who had challenged Steve Jobs. Every one of those award winners was promoted.

Cohesion and dissent sound contradictory, but a combination of the two is what brings novel ideas to the table—and keeps a strong culture from becoming a cult. Here are some ways to hold these principles in productive tension.

Prioritize organizational values

Give people a framework for choosing between conflicting opinions and allowing the best ideas to win out. When companies fail to prioritize values, performance suffers. My colleague Andrew Carton led a study showing that across hospitals, heart attack readmission rates were lower and returns on assets were higher when leaders articulated a compelling vision—but only if they spelled out no more than four organizational values. The more values they emphasized beyond that, the greater the odds that people interpreted them differently or didn't focus on the same ones.

Values need to be rank-ordered so that when employees face choices between competing courses of action, they know what comes first. At the software company Salesforce.com, trust is explicitly defined as the number one value, above growth and innovation. This value communicates a clear message to employees: When working on new software, never compromise data privacy. Tony Hsieh, the founder and longtime CEO of online shoe and clothing retailer Zappos, prioritized employee happiness over customer happiness. WestJet Airlines identifies safety as its most important value. And at Give-Forward, a company that helps people raise money for causes, compassion tops the list. Although media coverage is critical to the company's success, cofounder Ethan Austin notes, "We will not push a story in the media unless we are certain that the customer whose story we are sharing will benefit more than we do."

Once you've prioritized the values, keep scrutinizing them. Encourage new hires to challenge the company's standard way of doing things when they disagree with it. They're the ones with the freshest perspective; they haven't yet gone native. If they familiarize themselves with the culture before speaking up, they'll have already started marching to the same drummer. At Bridgewater, when new employees are trained, they're asked this question about the company's principles: "Do you disagree?"

Solicit problems, not just solutions

When working with executives, organizational psychologist David Hofmann likes to ask them to fill in the blanks in this sentence: "Don't bring me ___; bring me ___." Without fail, they shout out, "Don't bring me *problems*; bring me *solutions*!"

Although leaders love it when employees come up with solutions, there's an unintended consequence: Inquiry gets dampened. If you're always expected to have an answer ready, you'll arrive at meetings with your diagnosis complete, missing out on the chance to learn from a range of perspectives. This solutions orientation may be especially common in the United States: In a study comparing American and German decision groups, psychology professor Nale Lehmann-Willenbrock and her team found that the Germans made twice as many statements about problems and 30% fewer statements about solutions. "Americans are driven to find solutions quickly," the researchers observe, "often without a complete and thorough analysis of the problem."

When individual members of a group have different information, as is usually the case in organizations, it's smarter to get all the problems out there before pursuing solutions. At the digital music company Spotify, instead of working on projects, people organize around long-term business problems. "If they were easy to solve," chief technology officer Oskar Stål notes, "we would have solved them already. When we create a new team, people typically stay together on a business problem for at least a year. If it becomes successful, the team and mission will exist for a long time." Angi (formerly Angie's List) cofounder Angie Hicks holds weekly office hours to hear concerns from employees. And when Traaseth became the CEO of the Norwegian government's innovation efforts, she again used the speed-date approach to give employees a voice. To make sure she had full visibility into problems, she asked people to name their three biggest bottlenecks and what they would like to safeguard or change. Only after gathering problems across a tour of 14 offices did she begin implementing solutions.

Don't appoint devil's advocates—go find them

UC Berkeley psychologist Charlan Nemeth has found that assigning someone to play devil's advocate doesn't overcome confirmation bias. Though people may pay lip service to considering the counterargument, they'll stick to their own views in the end.

To make a difference, the devil's advocate has to actually hold a dissenting view, not just voice it for argument's sake, and the group has to believe that the dissent is authentic. Under those circumstances, groups look at more information *against* the majority view than for it, and they're less confident in their original preferences. Role-played disagreements are rarely argued forcefully or taken seriously; actual disagreement is what stimulates thought.

Groups with authentic dissenters generate more—and better—solutions to problems. Abraham Lincoln famously asked his political rivals to join his cabinet, knowing they would genuinely hold contrarian views. At one Berkshire Hathaway annual meeting, CEO Warren Buffett invited a trader who was shorting the stock to share his criticisms. Of course, this strategy works only if the dissenter's input is clearly valued and respected.

Model receptivity to critical feedback

Many managers end up promoting conformity because their egos are fragile. Research reveals that insecurity prevents managers from seeking ideas and leads them to respond defensively to suggestions. Employees quickly pick up on this attitude and withhold ideas to avoid trouble. One way to overcome this barrier is to encourage people to challenge you out in the open.

Years ago at the software company Index Group, CEO Tom Gerrity gathered his full staff of about 100 people and had a consultant give him negative feedback in front of everyone. When employees saw their CEO listen to critical opinions, they became less worried about speaking up. And managers themselves became more receptive to tough comments.

You can also encourage people to challenge you by broadcasting your weaknesses. Sheryl Sandberg, the longtime chief operating officer of Facebook, spoke to the 2012 graduating class at Harvard Business School about this challenge: "When you're the leader, it is really hard to get good and honest feedback, no matter how many times you ask for it. One trick I've discovered is that I try to speak really openly about the things I'm bad at, because that gives people permission to agree with me, which is a lot easier than pointing it out in the first place." For example, Sandberg tells her colleagues that she has a habit of talking too much in meetings. "If I never mentioned it, would anyone walk up to me and say, 'Hey, Sheryl, I think you talked too much today'? I doubt it."

For a culture of originality to flourish, employees must feel free to contribute their wildest ideas. But people are often afraid to speak up, even if they've never seen anything bad happen to those who do.

To fight that fear in the navy, Kohlmann rejected the military's traditional emphasis on hierarchy. Everyone communicated on a first-name basis, ignoring rank. "If you have an idea, pitch it to the crowd and run with it," he told members of his rapid-innovation cell. And he introduced them to people who had successfully championed creativity and change in the navy, to show them that innovation was possible.

Other ways to nip fear in the bud include applauding employees for speaking up, even when their suggestions don't get adopted, and sharing your own harebrained ideas. Without some degree of organizational tolerance for bad ideas, conformity will begin to rear its ugly head. Ultimately, listening to a wider range of insights than you normally hear is the key to promoting great original thinking.

If at first you don't succeed, you'll know you're aiming high enough.

———————

Adam Grant is an organizational psychologist at Wharton and the author of *Think Again: The Power of Knowing What You Don't Know.*

Index

Smart advice and inspiration from a source you trust.

If you enjoyed this book and want more comprehensive guidance on essential professional skills, turn to the HBR Guides Boxed Set. Packed with the practical advice you need to succeed, this seven-volume collection provides smart answers to your most pressing work challenges, from writing more effective emails and delivering persuasive presentations to setting priorities and managing up and across.

Harvard Business Review Guides

Available in paperback or ebook format. Plus, find downloadable tools and templates to help you get started.

- Better Business Writing
- Building Your Business Case
- Buying a Small Business
- Coaching Employees
- Delivering Effective Feedback
- Finance Basics for Managers
- Getting the Mentoring You Need
- Getting the Right Work Done

- Leading Teams
- Making Every Meeting Matter
- Managing Stress at Work
- Managing Up and Across
- Negotiating
- Office Politics
- Persuasive Presentations
- Project Management

HBR.ORG/GUIDES

Buy for your team, clients, or event.
Visit hbr.org/bulksales for quantity discount rates.

Notes

Notes

Notes

Notes

Notes